THE BOOK OF

Cheesecakes

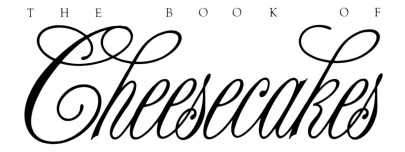

THE BOOK OF

Cheesecakes

STEVEN WHEELER

Photography by
PAUL GRATER

HPBooks

ANOTHER BEST SELLING VOLUME FROM HPBooks

HPBooks
A division of Price Stern Sloan, Inc.
360 North La Cienega Boulevard
Los Angeles, California 90048
9 8 7 6 5 4 3 2

By arrangement with Salamander Books Ltd. and Merehurst Press, London.

Home Economist : Steven Wheeler
Color separation by J. Film Process Ltd., Bangkok, Thailand
Printed in Belgium by Proost International Book Production

Second Printing

Library of Congress Cataloging-in-Publication Data

Wheeler, Steven.
   The book of cheesecakes.

   Includes index.
   1. Cheesecake (Cookery)   I. Title.
TX773.W485   1988   641.8'65   87-21252
ISBN 0-89586-668-4

CONTENTS

STEVEN WHEELER

A young and newly discovered author, Steven Wheeler's professional experience to date is certainly impressive. He has lectured at La Petite Cuisine School of Cookery and The Jane Mann School of Cookery. Steven is a trained pastry chef who has worked in hotels and restaurants in Switzerland and England, including The Dorchester Hotel in London. He contributes articles to magazines and is the author of *Natural Desserts*.

INTRODUCTION

Sinfully delicious, cheesecakes are guaranteed to win favor with all guests, young and old. Hosts and hostesses have been known to earn their entire culinary reputation from the success of one cheesecake. No other dessert invokes so much talk about secret ingredients, specials crusts and toppings. *The Book of Cheesecakes* is a collection of a hundred fantastic recipes for this most luxurious of treats. It includes my personal versions of classics such as the Russian Easter Cheesecake, Paskha and New York's favorite, Lindy's Cheesecake, as well as a whole range of others including fruit cheesecakes, chocolate cheesecakes, ones made with spices, wine or spirits, low-fat ones and individual cheesecakes.

Many are suitable for lunch and dinner parties, others can be enjoyed at tea or coffee time. Also included are a number of savory cheesecakes which make deliciously different starters or main courses.

Every recipe is photographed in full color and there are step-by-step instructions for making unusual spongecake borders, both plain and chocolate striped, and special cheesecake pastries which make a firm crust for the rich cream fillings.

The Book of Cheesecakes will enable you to entertain in style, producing elegant desserts with a minimum of work and effort.

EQUIPMENT

The great advantage of a cheesecake is the ease with which it can be put together. Cheesecakes in this book use a minimum of equipment.

Wooden spoon and mixing bowl: Most of the cheesecake fillings are simple mixtures of cheese, whipping cream and eggs beaten in a bowl with a wooden spoon, then spooned into a pastry shell or crumb crust.

Blender or food processor: A blender or food processor can be used to mix the fillings, if desired, and will give a very light texture. They are also useful for making fruit purees and crushing cookies. Or, cookies or wafers can be put into a strong plastic bag and crushed with a rolling pin.

Springform pans: These removable bottom pans are particularly good for cheesecakes. They have a spring clip which releases the sides, allowing the cheesecake to be removed easily.

Terrines: These can be used to give a different shaped cheesecake, but are only suitable for ones that are inverted when removed from the pan.

Other shapes: The traditional mold for Paskha is a clay flower pot. For Coeurs à la Crème, special heart-shaped molds are needed.

Baking Sheets: Baking sheets are needed for roulades where the filling is spread on a prepared spongecake and rolled up, jelly-roll fashion.

Pastry bag and nozzles: These are used for piping the fancy spongecake borders and piping whipped cream to decorate the cheesecakes.

CHEESES

All the sweet cheesecakes in this book are made with fresh or unripened cheeses. These are spreadable cheeses and have soft textures and mild flavors. The fat content of soft cheeses varies considerably. The cheeses may be lumpy with curds, smooth and creamy or molded in firm blocks. Some of the savory cheesecakes use other stronger-flavored cheeses such as Gruyère, Parmesan or goat cheese.

Cream cheese: Cream cheese has a fat content of 33% or more. Cream cheese was first developed in the United States by combining whole milk and cream. A method perfected in 1945 produces a fine-textured, smooth-bodied cheese that keeps well.

Neufchâtel: Neufchâtel is similar to cream cheese, but has a 22% fat content. It also has a mild flavor and smooth, creamy texture.

Cottage Cheese: Cottage cheese is made from skim milk. It may be purchased dry or creamed with a mixture of cream and milk. Fat content may be very low or medium, depending on what has been added to it. It has large soft curds and needs sieving before using in a cheesecake.

Ricotta cheese: Ricotta cheese, the Italian equivalent of cottage cheese, has a smooth texture and mild, sweet flavor. It is traditionally made from whey rather than curds, but may have full or skimmed milk added to it to make a richer cheese. Fat content varies from low to medium.

Mascarpone: Mascarpone looks like a thick velvety cream, but is sweeter. It has a fat content of 45% to 55%.

—— PLAIN SPONGECAKE BORDER ——

3 eggs, room temperature
3 tablespoons sugar
1/4 cup all-purpose flour

Preheat oven to 425F (220C). Line a baking sheet with waxed paper. Beat eggs and sugar in a large bowl until they are thick and foamy and hold a ribbon when drawn over surface.

Sift flour over eggs and fold in carefully. Using minimal pressure, pipe (with a pastry bag fitted with a 1/2-inch nozzle) lines of spongecake batter across short side of baking sheet, just touching each other. Bake in preheated oven on top rack 10 to 12 minutes or until springy to touch.

Spread a tea towel on a flat surface. Pick spongecake up by waxed paper and place upside down on tea towel; this will prevent spongecake drying. Cool and cut in strips to depth of cheesecake pan. Leave waxed paper on spongecake until used. Freeze up to 12 weeks.

CHOCOLATE STRIPE SPONGECAKE BORDER

3 eggs, room temperature
3 tablespoons sugar
1/4 cup all-purpose flour
1 tablespoon unsweetened cocoa
powder

Preheat oven to 425F (220C). Line a baking sheet with waxed paper. Beat eggs and sugar in a large bowl until they are thick and foamy and hold a ribbon when drawn over surface.

Divide mixture between 2 small bowls. Sift 2 tablespoons of flour over 1 bowl and fold in carefully. Using minimal pressure, pipe (with a pastry bag fitted with a 1/2-inch nozzle) as many lines of spongecake batter as possible across short side of baking sheet, 1 finger-width apart.

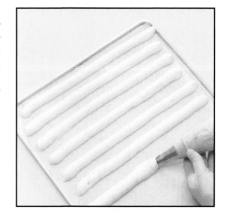

Sift remaining 2 tablespoons of flour and cocoa over remaining egg mixture and fold in as before. Pipe (using same pastry bag) chocolate spongecake mixture in between lines already piped. Bake in preheated oven on top rack 10 to 12 minutes or until spongecake is springy to touch. Spread a tea towel on a flat surface. Pick spongecake up by waxed paper and place upside down on tea towel; this will prevent spongecake drying. Cool and cut in strips to depth of cheesecake pan. Leave waxed paper on spongecake until used. Freeze up to 12 weeks.

— SPECIAL CHEESECAKE PASTRY —

3/4 cup all-purpose flour
1/2 cup self-rising flour
1/4 cup sugar
1/2 cup lightly salted butter, chilled,
   cut in pieces
2 egg yolks

Sift flours into a large bowl or food processor. Stir in sugar.

Cut butter into flour with 2 knives or a pastry blender until mixture resembles cornmeal. Or, process in food processor 1 minute.

Add egg yolks and stir with a fork until dough forms. If dough feels soft, refrigerate until butter firms. Store in refrigerator up to 4 days. Bring pastry to room temperature before using. Makes enough dough to line a 9-inch springform pan.

—— SWEET SHORTCRUST PASTRY ——

1-3/4 cups all-purpose flour
2 tablespoons powdered sugar
1/2 cup butter or margarine, chilled,
   cut in pieces
1 egg
1/2 teaspoon vanilla extract

Sift flour and powdered sugar into a
large bowl or food processor.

Add butter; cut into flour with 2
knives or a pastry blender until mixture resembles cornmeal. Or, process
in food processor about 45 seconds.

Add egg and vanilla. Stir with a fork
until dough forms. Cover with plastic
wrap and refrigerate 1 hour before
using. Store in refrigerator up to 4
days or freeze up to 6 weeks. Makes
enough dough to line a 9-inch
springform pan.

—— AMARETTI CHEESECAKE ——

Crust:
1/4 cup butter
1/2 cup crushed vanilla wafers
1 cup soft macaroon pieces

Filling:
1 lb. Neufchâtel cheese, softened
2/3 cup sour cream
1/3 cup plus 3 tablespoons sugar
3 eggs, separated
1 tablespoon all-purpose flour
1/2 teaspoon almond extract
Finely grated peel and juice of 1
  lemon

Garnish:
1 (16-oz.) can apricot halves, drained
2/3 cup whipping cream

Grease a 9-inch springform pan. To prepare crust, melt butter in a small saucepan over low heat. Stir in crushed vanilla wafers and macaroon pieces. Press mixture in bottom of greased pan. Set aside. To prepare filling, beat Neufchâtel cheese, sour cream and 1/3 cup sugar in a large bowl until smooth. Stir in egg yolks, flour, almond extract and lemon peel and juice. Beat egg whites with remaining sugar until soft peaks form; fold into cheese mixture. Spoon filling into prepared crust. Refrigerate 2 to 3 hours or until set. Remove from pan. To garnish, arrange apricot halves on cheesecake. Whip cream until stiff. Pipe (with a pastry bag) small whipped cream rosettes in between each apricot half and chill before serving. Makes 12 servings.

—— BLACK FOREST CHEESECAKE ——

Crust:
1/3 cup butter
1-1/2 cups crushed vanilla wafers

Filling:
1-1/2 lb. cream cheese, softened
3 eggs
2/3 cup sugar
1/2 (16-1/2-oz.) can black cherries, drained
2 tablespoons unsweetened cocoa powder
1 teaspoon ground cinnamon
1/3 cup whipping cream
4 oz. unsweetened chocolate, broken in pieces

Topping:
1 (16-oz.) can black cherries, drained, juice reserved
1 tablespoon plus 1 teaspoon cornstarch
2 tablespoons water

Preheat oven to 350F (175C). Grease an 8- or 9-inch springform pan. To prepare crust, melt butter in a small saucepan over low heat. Stir in crushed vanilla wafers. Press mixture in bottom of greased pan. Set aside. To prepare filling, beat cream cheese, eggs and sugar in a medium-size bowl until smooth. Spoon 1/2 of filling into prepared crust. Spoon drained cherries over filling. Stir cocoa and cinnamon into remaining half of filling. Bring whipping cream to a simmer in a small saucepan over low heat. Stir in chocolate until melted; cool. Stir chocolate mixture into remaining half of filling; pour over cherries. Bake in preheated oven 35 to 45 minutes or just until set. To prepare topping, pour reserved cherry juice into a small saucepan and bring to a boil. Combine cornstarch and water; stir into cherry juice. Simmer until thickened. Stir in cherries. Pour over cooked cheesecake. Refrigerate until topping is set. Makes 8 to 10 servings.

CHERRY CHEESE STRUDEL

Filling:
3/4 cup ricotta cheese
1/2 cup cottage cheese, sieved
1/4 cup sour cream
3 tablespoons ground almonds
1/3 cup butter
2 cups fresh bread crumbs
2 teaspoons all-purpose flour
8 sheets filo pastry
1/2 cup butter, melted
1 (16-oz.) can black cherries, drained
1/3 cup packed brown sugar

Garnish:
Powdered sugar

Preheat oven to 400F (205C). To prepare filling, beat ricotta cheese, cottage cheese and sour cream in a medium-size bowl until smooth. Stir in almonds. Set aside. Melt 1/3 cup butter in a large skillet over medium heat and fry bread crumbs until golden. Set aside. Spread a tea towel on counter and dust with flour. Working quickly, lay a sheet of pastry on tea towel and brush lightly with melted butter. Cover with a second sheet of pastry and repeat until all pastry is used. Spoon filling over pastry, leaving a 1-inch border on all sides. Spoon drained cherries over filling. Sprinkle bread crumbs and brown sugar over cherries. Roll lengthwise, jelly-roll fashion. Place on a baking sheet. Brush surface with melted butter. Bake in preheated oven 40 minutes or until golden brown. Cool. To garnish, dust with powdered sugar. Makes 8 servings.

—— CONTINENTAL CHEESECAKE ——

Crust:
1 recipe Sweet Shortcake Pastry,
   page 13

Filling:
1 lb. cottage cheese, sieved
2/3 cup whipping cream
3 eggs, separated
Scant 1/2 cup sugar
1/2 cup ground almonds
Finely grated peel and juice of 1
   lemon
1/3 cup chopped candied citrus peel
1/3 cup raisins

Glaze:
1 egg yolk
1/4 teaspoon salt

Preheat oven to 375F (190C). Grease an 11" x 7" baking pan. To prepare crust, on a lightly floured surface, roll Sweet Shortcake Pastry to a 1/4-inch thickness. Line greased pan with dough. Fill dough with dried beans or dried pasta. Bake in preheated oven 20 minutes or until lightly browned. Remove beans and cool. Reduce oven to 350F (175C). To prepare filling, beat cottage cheese, whipping cream and egg yolks until smooth. Add 1/4 cup plus 2 tablespoons of sugar, almonds and lemon peel and juice. Beat until smooth. Stir in citrus peel and raisins. Beat egg whites with remaining sugar until soft peaks form; fold into cheese mixture. Spoon filling into prepared crust. Place strips of leftover pastry on cheesecake. To prepare glaze, beat egg yolk and salt. Brush strips of pastry with beaten egg yolk. Bake in preheated oven 40 minutes. Cool completely. Cut cheesecake in bars. Makes 10 to 12 servings.

KASTOBERSTORTE

Spongecake Top & Bottom:
2 eggs
3 tablespoons sugar
2 tablespoons all-purpose flour
2 tablespoons cornstarch

Filling:
4 oz. cream cheese, softened
1/2 cup cottage cheese, sieved
2/3 cup plain yogurt
1/3 cup raisins
Finely grated peel and juice of 1 orange
2/3 cup whipping cream, whipped
1 tablespoon gelatin
2 tablespoons water
2 eggs
2 tablespoons honey

Garnish:
Powdered sugar

Preheat oven to 400F (205C). Grease 2 baking sheets and line with parchment paper. Trace a 9-inch circle on each sheet. To prepare spongecake bottom and top, beat eggs and sugar until they are thick and foamy and hold a ribbon when drawn over surface. Sift flour and cornstarch over egg mixture and fold in. Spoon spongecake mixture on baking sheets; spread beyond traced circles. Bake in preheated oven 12 to 15 minutes with oven door ajar 1/2 inch. Cool completely. To prepare filling, beat cream cheese, cottage cheese and yogurt in a large bowl until smooth. Stir in raisins and orange peel and juice. Fold in whipped cream. Combine gelatin and water in a small saucepan. Simmer until gelatin is completely dissolved; stir into cheese mixture. Beat eggs and honey until they are thick and foamy and hold a ribbon when drawn over surface; fold into cheese mixture. To assemble, trim spongecakes to a diameter of 9 inches. Place 1 spongecake in a 9-inch springform pan. Spoon filling over spongecake in pan. Refrigerate 2 to 3 hours or until set. Place remaining spongecake on filling. To garnish, dust with powdered sugar. Makes 8 to 10 servings.

– MIDDLE EASTERN CHEESE SLICES –

Filling:
1-1/2 cups cottage cheese, sieved
2/3 cup buttermilk
4 eggs
1/4 cup butter, melted
2 tablespoons honey
2 tablespoons sugar
1-1/4 cups self-rising flour

Syrup:
3/4 cup sugar
1 teaspoon orange flower water
2/3 cup water

Garnish
Orange segments
Orange peel strips

Preheat oven to 375F (190C). Grease an 8-inch-square baking pan and line with parchment paper. To prepare filling, beat cottage cheese, buttermilk, eggs, butter, honey, sugar and flour until smooth. Spoon filling into greased pan. Bake in preheated oven 35 minutes or until set. To prepare syrup, combine sugar, orange flower water and water in a saucepan. Bring to a boil, reduce heat and simmer until sugar dissolves. While cheesecake is still warm, pour syrup over cake. Cool completely. To serve, cut cheesecake in small bars. Garnish with orange segments and strips of orange peel. Makes 8 to 10 servings.

PASKHA

Filling:
1-1/2 lb. ricotta cheese
2/3 cup sour cream
1/3 cup unsalted butter, softened
1/3 cup sugar
2 tablespoons honey
1 tablespoon rose water
1/2 cup ground almonds
1/2 cup seedless raisins
1/2 cup chopped candied citrus peel
1/3 cup chopped glacé cherries

Garnish:
Glacè cherries

Line a new 6-cup capacity clay flower pot with 2 layers of cheese cloth or muslin so cloth overlaps edges by 2 inches. To prepare filling, beat ricotta cheese, sour cream and butter in a large bowl until smooth. Stir in sugar, honey, rose water, almonds, raisins, citrus peel and cherries. Spoon filling into lined flower pot and fold edges of cheese cloth to center. Place flower pot on a saucer; place a smaller saucer inside of flower pot. Put a brick, large canned good or other weight on top saucer 24 hours. Turn cheese out on a serving dish. Garnish with glacé cherries. Makes 8 to 10 servings.

— POLISH FESTIVAL CHEESECAKE —

Crust:
1 recipe Sweet Shortcrust Pastry,
page 13

Filling:
1-1/2 lb. ricotta cheese
2/3 cup whipping cream
Scant 1/2 cup sugar
1 tablespoon all-purpose flour
3 eggs
2 tablespoons golden raisins
1 tablespoon orange flower water

Preheat oven to 400F (205C). Grease a 9-inch springform pan. To prepare crust, on a lightly floured surface, roll Sweet Shortcrust Pastry to a 1/8-inch thickness. Line greased pan with dough. Set aside. To prepare filling, beat ricotta cheese, whipping cream, sugar, flour and eggs in a large bowl until smooth. Stir in raisins and orange flower water. Spoon filling into prepared dough. Decorate with strips of leftover pastry arranged in a crisscross pattern. Bake in preheated oven 20 minutes. Reduce oven to 350 (175C) and bake 45 minutes more or until set. Cool before removing from pan. Makes 10 to 12 servings.

—— PRUNE CHEESECAKE ——

Filling:
1-1/2 cups pitted prunes
1/2 cup Armagnac or brandy
8 oz. cream cheese, softened
1 cup cottage cheese, sieved
1-1/4 cups sour cream
2 eggs
Scant 1/2 cup sugar
2 tablespoons all-purpose flour

Crust:
1-3/4 cups crushed chocolate wafers
1/4 cup ground walnuts
1/3 cup butter

Garnish:
Powdered sugar

To prepare filling, place prunes in a bowl and cover with boiling water. Soak 15 minutes. Drain and discard water. Combine prunes and Armagnac. Cover with plastic wrap and let stand at room temperature 24 hours. Preheat oven to 350F (175C). Grease an 8-inch springform pan. To prepare crust, melt butter in a small saucepan over low heat. Stir in crushed chocolate wafers and walnuts. Press mixture in bottom of greased pan. Set aside. Drain and reserve liquid from prunes. Reserve 5 prunes for decoration. Coarsely chop remaining prunes. Beat cream cheese, cottage cheese, sour cream and eggs in a medium-size bowl until smooth. Beat in sugar and flour. Stir chopped prunes into cheese mixture. Stir in 1/2 of reserved prune liquid. Spoon filling into prepared crust. Bake in preheated oven 45 minutes or until set. Cool before removing from pan. To garnish, dust with powdered sugar. Cut reserved prunes in half and arrange on cheesecake. Makes 8 to 10 servings.

———— RUSSIAN VATROUCHKA ————

Crust:
**1 recipe Sweet Shortcake Pastry,
page 13**

Filling:
**8 oz. cream cheese, softened
1 cup cottage cheese, sieved
1/2 cup powdered sugar
1/3 cup butter, softened
1/3 cup whipping cream
1 tablespoon all-purpose flour
1 egg
1/2 cup toasted slivered almonds
1/2 cup chopped walnuts
1/2 cup chopped mixed glacé fruits
1/3 cup raisins**

Garnish:
Powdered sugar

Preheat oven to 350F (175C). Grease a 9-inch springform pan. To prepare crust, on a lightly floured surface, roll Sweet Shortcake Pastry to a 1/4-inch thickness. Line greased pan with dough. Set aside. To prepare filling, beat cream cheese, cottage cheese, powdered sugar, butter and whipping cream in a large bowl. Beat in flour and egg until smooth. Stir in almonds, walnuts, glacé fruits and raisins. Spoon filling into prepared dough. Bake in preheated oven 50 minutes or until set. Cool completely before removing from pan. To garnish, dust with powdered sugar. Makes 10 to 12 servings.

CITRUS CHEESECAKE

Crust:
1/4 cup butter
2 cups graham cracker crumbs

Filling:
7 oz. Neufchâtel cheese, softened
2/3 cup plain yogurt
Finely grated peel of 2 oranges
Finely grated peel of 2 lemons
2/3 cup whipping cream, whipped
4 teaspoons unflavored gelatin
2 tablespoons water
2 eggs
2 tablespoons honey

Topping:
3 oranges
Juice of 2 lemons
1/4 cup sugar
1 tablespoon cornstarch
1/4 cup water
1 kiwifruit
3/4 cup seedless black grapes

Grease an 8-inch springform pan and line with waxed paper. To prepare crust, melt butter in a small saucepan over low heat. Stir in graham cracker crumbs. Press mixture in bottom of greased pan. Set aside. To prepare filling, beat Neufchâtel cheese, yogurt and citrus peel in a large bowl until smooth. Fold whipped cream into cheese mixture. Combine gelatin and water in a small saucepan. Simmer until gelatin is completely dissolved; stir into cheese mixture. In a small bowl, beat eggs and honey until they are thick and foamy and hold a ribbon when drawn over surface; fold into cheese mixture. Spoon filling into prepared crust. Refrigerate 2 to 3 hours or until set. To prepare topping, peel and cut oranges in segments. Catch juices in a small saucepan. Reserve orange segments. Add lemon juice to orange juice. Stir in sugar and bring to a boil. Combine cornstarch with water; stir into citrus juice. Simmer until thickened; cool. When cheesecake has set, spread topping on cheesecake. Cool completely before removing from pan. Peel and slice kiwifruit. Slice grapes. Arrange orange segments, kiwifruit and grapes on cheesecake. Makes 8 servings.

COTTAGE CHEESECAKE

Crust:
1/2 cup butter
2 tablespoons light-brown sugar
2/3 cup regular rolled oats

Filling:
1 lb. cottage cheese, sieved
2/3 cup sour cream
2 ripe bananas, peeled, mashed
1/3 cup packed light-brown sugar
2 eggs
2 tablespoons all-purpose flour
1/2 teaspoon vanilla extract

Preheat oven to 350F (175C). Grease an 8-inch springform pan. To prepare crust, melt butter in a small saucepan over low heat. Stir in brown sugar and oats. Spread 1/2 of crust mixture in greased pan. Set aside. To prepare filling, beat cottage cheese, sour cream, bananas, brown sugar, eggs, flour and vanilla until smooth. Spoon filling into prepared crust. Sprinkle with remaining crust mixture. Bake in preheated oven 50 minutes or until set. Cool before removing from pan. Makes 8 to 10 servings.

APPLE CHEESECAKE

Crust:
**1 recipe Special Cheesecake Pastry,
page 12**

Filling:
**1 lb. cottage cheese, sieved
2/3 cup sour cream
Scant 1/2 cup sugar
2 eggs
1 tablespoon all-purpose flour
Pinch of ground cinnamon
Finely grated peel and juice of 1
lemon
1 lb. apples, peeled, cored, finely
chopped**

Topping:
**2-1/2 cups bran flakes
2 tablespoons powdered sugar**

Preheat oven to 375F (190C). Grease a 9-inch pie pan. To prepare crust, on a lightly floured surface, roll Special Cheesecake Pastry to a 1/4-inch thickness. Line greased pan with dough. Prick dough with a fork. Refrigerate while preparing filling. To prepare filling, beat cottage cheese, sour cream, sugar, eggs, flour and cinnamon until smooth. Stir in lemon peel and juice. Spread 1/2 of apples in prepared dough. Pour filling over apples. Top with remaining apples. To prepare topping, combine bran flakes and 1 tablespoon of powdered sugar in a small bowl. Sprinkle over apples. Bake in preheated oven 45 minutes or until set. Cool completely. Dust with remaining powdered sugar. Makes 8 to 10 servings.

—— BUTTERMILK CHEESECAKE ——

Crust:
1/3 cup butter
1-3/4 cups crushed vanilla wafers

Filling:
1 lb. ricotta cheese
1/2 cup buttermilk
2 eggs
Scant 1/2 cup sugar
1 teaspoon vanilla extract
1 tablespoon all-purpose flour

Topping:
1-3/4 cups plain yogurt

Garnish:
Twists of lemon peel

Preheat oven to 325F (165C). Grease an 8-inch springform pan. To prepare crust, melt butter in a small saucepan over low heat. Stir in crushed vanilla wafers. Press mixture in bottom of greased pan. Set aside. To prepare filling, beat ricotta cheese and 1/4 cup of buttermilk in a large bowl. Add remaining 1/4 cup of buttermilk and beat until smooth. Beat in eggs, sugar, vanilla and flour. Spoon filling into prepared crust. Bake in preheated oven 50 minutes or until set. Cool before removing from pan. Spread yogurt on cheesecake. Garnish edge of cheesecake with twists of lemon peel. Makes 8 to 10 servings.

—— TOFU-BANANA CHEESECAKE ——

Crust:
1/4 cup butter
1 cup crushed vanilla wafers

Filling:
12 oz. tofu, cut in 1/2-inch pieces
1-1/2 cups cottage cheese, sieved
2 ripe bananas, peeled, mashed
1 tablespoon honey
1 tablespoon all-purpose flour
Finely grated peel and juice of 1 lime

Garnish:
2 bananas
1/4 cup apricot jam
1 tablespoon lemon juice
Angelica pieces, cut in "leaves"

Preheat oven to 350F (175C). Grease an 8-inch springform pan. To prepare crust, melt butter in a small saucepan over low heat. Stir in crushed vanilla wafers. Press mixture in bottom of greased pan. Set aside. To prepare filling, beat tofu, cottage cheese, bananas, honey, flour and lime peel and juice until smooth. Spoon filling into prepared crust. Bake in preheated oven 45 minutes or until set. To garnish, slice bananas diagonally in ovals. Arrange slices around edge of cheesecake. Heat apricot jam and lemon juice in a small saucepan over low heat until mixture liquifies. Brush bananas with glaze. Arrange angelica "leaves" on banana slices. Makes 8 to 10 servings.

BLACKBERRY & APPLE CHEESECAKE

Crust:
1/2 cup butter
2 tablespoons light-brown sugar
2 cups regular rolled oats

Filling:
1 lb. ricotta cheese
2/3 cup sour cream
Scant 1/2 cup sugar
2 eggs
1 tablespoon all-purpose flour
Pinch ground cloves
1 lb. apples, peeled, cored, coarsely chopped
1/2 cup fresh or thawed frozen blackberries

Garnish:
2 cups fresh blackberries
1/3 cup red currant jelly
2/3 cup whipping cream
8 to 10 fresh mint sprigs

Preheat oven to 350F (175C). Grease an 8-inch springform pan. To prepare crust, melt butter in a small saucepan over low heat. Stir in brown sugar and oats. Press mixture in bottom of greased pan. Set aside. To prepare filling, beat ricotta cheese, sour cream, sugar and eggs until smooth. Beat in flour and cloves. Stir apples and blackberries into cheese mixture. Spoon filling into prepared crust. Bake in preheated oven 45 minutes or until set. Cool completely before removing from pan. To garnish, arrange blackberries in center of cheesecake. Heat red currant jelly in a small saucepan until it liquifies; brush over blackberries. Whip cream until stiff. Pipe (with a pastry bag) a border of 8 to 10 whipped cream rosettes around edge of cheesecake. Top each rosette with a sprig of mint. Makes 8 to 10 servings.

PLUM CHEESECAKE

Crust:
**1 recipe Special Cheesecake Pastry,
page 12**

Filling:
**7 oz. ricotta cheese
1 egg
1/4 cup sugar
2/3 cup plain yogurt
1 tablespoon lemon juice
1/2 teaspoon ground cinnamon
1 lb. red plums, cut in half, seeded**

Topping:
**2 tablespoons firm butter
1/2 cup all-purpose flour
2 tablespoons light-brown sugar**

Preheat oven to 350F (175C). Grease an 8-inch pie pan. To prepare crust, on a lightly floured surface, roll Special Cheesecake Pastry to a 1/4-inch thickness. Line greased pan with dough. Prick dough with a fork. Refrigerate while preparing filling. To prepare filling, beat riccotta cheese, egg, sugar and yogurt in a large bowl. Add lemon juice and cinnamon; beat until smooth. Arrange 1/2 of plum halves in prepared dough. Spread with cheese mixture. Cover with remaining plum halves. To make topping, using 2 knives or a pastry blender, cut butter into flour and sugar until mixture resembles coarse bread crumbs. Sprinkle over plums. Bake in preheated oven 50 minutes. Cool before cutting. Makes 6 to 8 servings.

DUBLIN CURD CAKE

Crust:
1 recipe Special Cheesecake Pastry,
  page 12

Filling:
6 oz. cream cheese, softened
3/4 cup cottage cheese, sieved
2/3 cup sour cream
1/4 cup sugar
2 eggs
1 tablespoon all-purpose flour
1/4 cup butter, melted

Topping:
1/2 cup raisins

Preheat oven to 375F (190C). Grease a 9-inch pie pan. To prepare crust, on a lightly floured surface, roll Special Cheesecake Pastry to a 1/4-inch thickness. Line greased pan with dough. Prick dough with a fork. Refrigerate while preparing filling. Beat cream cheese, cottage cheese, sour cream, sugar and eggs in a large bowl. Add flour and melted butter; beat until smooth. Spoon filling into prepared dough. Sprinkle with raisins. Bake in preheated oven 40 minutes. Serve warm or cold. Makes 8 servings.

————— GINGER CURD CAKE —————

Crust:
1/4 cup butter
1-3/4 cups crushed gingersnaps

Fillings:
12 oz. cream cheese, softened
1-1/2 cups cottage cheese, sieved
2 eggs
3 tablespoons honey
2 tablespoons stem ginger syrup
Finely grated peel and juice of 1
    orange

Garnish:
8 to 10 pieces stem ginger
Angelica pieces, cut in "leaves"

Preheat oven to 325F (165C). Grease a 9-inch springform pan. To prepare crust, melt butter in a small saucepan over low heat. Stir in crushed gingersnaps. Press mixture in greased pan. Set aside. To prepare filling, beat cream cheese, cottage cheese, eggs, honey, ginger syrup and orange peel and juice in a medium-size bowl until smooth. Spoon filling into prepared crust. Bake in pre-heated oven 1-1/4 hours or until set. Cool before removing from pan. To garnish, slice each piece of stem ginger in 5 pieces. Arrange ginger slices in groups of 5 for each serving. Place angelica "leaves" on ginger slices. Makes 8 to 10 servings.

RHUBARB & CUSTARD CHEESECAKE

Crust:
1/4 cup butter
1-3/4 cups crushed gingersnaps

Filling:
2 tablespoons cornstarch
1 cup milk
3 egg yolks
1/2 teaspoon vanilla extract
2 tablespoons sugar
4 teaspoons unflavored gelatin
2 tablespoons water
12 oz. Neufchâtel cheese, softened

Topping:
2 lb. fresh rhubarb, cut in 2-1/2-inch
   pieces
Scant 1/2 cup sugar
2-1/2 cups boiling water

Garnish:
8 sprigs fresh mint

Grease a 9-inch springform pan. To prepare crust, melt butter in a small saucepan over low heat. Stir in crushed gingersnaps. Press mixture in bottom of greased pan. Set aside. To prepare filling, combine cornstarch with 3 tablespoons of milk in a large glass bowl. Beat in egg yolks and vanilla. Bring remaining milk to boil in a small saucepan. Pour into egg yolk mixture and stir well. Return mixture to saucepan. Stir in sugar and simmer until thickened; remove from heat. Combine gelatin and water in a small saucepan. Simmer until gelatin is completely dissolved; stir into thickened custard. Cool custard until almost set. Beat Neufchâtel cheese, a little at a time, into custard. Spoon filling into prepared crust. Refrigerate 2 to 3 hours or until set. To prepare topping, combine rhubard, sugar and water in a saucepan. Simmer covered, stirring occasionally, 25 to 30 minutes or until rhubarb is just tender. Remove cheesecake from pan. Drain rhubarb slices and arrange in a fan shape around edge of cheesecake. Overlap a second layer. Chill cheesecake. Garnish with sprigs of mint. Makes 8 servings.

CAROUSEL DE FROMAGE

Filling:
1 lb. Neufchâtel cheese, softened
1-1/4 cups whipping cream
Scant 1/2 cup sugar
3 eggs
1 teaspoon vanilla extract

Topping:
2 tart green cooking apples
2 pears
2 oranges
1 kiwifruit
1 pint basket strawberries
1 pint basket raspberries
3/4 cup seedless black grapes

Garnish:
2/3 cup whipping cream
8 to 10 sprigs fresh mint

Preheat oven to 375F (190C). Grease a 9-inch ring mold. To prepare filling, beat Neufchâtel cheese and whipping cream in a large bowl until smooth. Beat in sugar, eggs and vanilla. Spoon filling into greased mold; place in a large roasting pan. Add enough boiling water to reach half way up side of mold. Cover roasting pan with foil. Bake in preheated oven 50 minutes or until a knife inserted just off center comes out clean. Cool before removing from mold. To prepare topping, cut apples, pears, oranges and kiwifruit in even-sized pieces. Arrange fruit in center of ring. To garnish, whip cream until stiff. Pipe (with a pastry bag) a border of 8 to 10 whipped cream rosettes around edge of cheesecake. Top each rosette with a sprig of mint. Makes 8 to 10 servings.

─ OLD-FASHIONED CHEESECAKE ─

Crust:
1/2 cup butter
1/4 cup packed brown sugar
1 cup whole-wheat flour
1 cup regular rolled oats

Filling:
12 oz. Neufchâtel cheese, softened
1-1/4 cups buttermilk
2 eggs
1/4 cup packed brown sugar
1 tablespoon all-purpose flour
1 teaspoon baking soda

Topping:
3/4 cup soft macaroon pieces

Preheat oven to 375F (190C). Grease an 8-inch pie pan. To prepare crust, melt butter in a small saucepan over low heat. Stir in brown sugar, flour and oats. Press mixture in greased pan. Set aside. To prepare filling, beat Neufchâtel cheese, buttermilk, eggs and brown sugar in a large bowl until smooth. Sift flour and baking soda. Stir into cheese mixture. Spoon filling into prepared crust. Sprinkle with macaroon pieces. Bake in pre-heated oven 35 minutes or until set. Cool before cutting. Makes 6 to 8 servings.

—— RICED-TOP CHEESECAKE ——

Crust:
1/2 cup butter
2-1/4 cups crushed vanilla wafers

Filling:
1 lb. Neufchâtel cheese, softened
2/3 cup whipping cream
Scant 1/2 cup sugar
2 eggs
1/2 cup chopped dried apricots

Topping:
3/4 cup butter, softened
1/2 cup sugar
1 egg
1/2 teaspoon vanilla extract
2-3/4 cups all-purpose flour

Garnish:
Powdered sugar

Preheat oven to 350F (175C). Grease an 8-inch springform pan. To prepare crust, melt butter in a small saucepan over low heat. Stir in crushed vanilla wafers. Press mixture in greased pan. Set aside. To prepare filling, beat Neufchâtel cheese, whipping cream, sugar and eggs in a large bowl until smooth. Stir in dried apricots. Spoon filling into prepared crust. Bake in preheated oven 30 minutes. To prepare topping, beat butter and sugar until pale in color. Gradually beat in egg. Add vanilla. Stir in flour. Force topping through a ricer over partially baked cheesecake, or crumble topping and sprinkle over partially baked cheesecake. Bake 20 minutes or until set. Cool before removing from pan. To garnish, dust with powdered sugar. Makes 8 to 10 servings.

MARBLED CHEESECAKE

Crust:
1/4 cup butter
1-3/4 cups graham cracker crumbs

Filling:
1-1/2 lb. Neufchâtel cheese, softened
Scant 1/2 cup sugar
1 tablespoon all-purpose flour
3 eggs
1 teaspoon vanilla extract
3 oz. semisweet chocolate, broken in pieces

Preheat oven to 350F (175C). Grease an 8-inch springform pan. To prepare crust, melt butter in a small saucepan over low heat. Stir in graham cracker crumbs. Press mixture in bottom of greased pan. Set aside. To prepare filling, beat Neufchâtel cheese, sugar, flour, eggs and vanilla in a medium-size bowl until smooth. Spoon filling into prepared crust. Melt chocolate in top of a double boiler or a bowl set over a pan of simmering water. Pour melted chocolate in a thin stream over cheese mixture. Using handle of a teaspoon, swirl to combine 2 mixtures to achieve a marbled effect. Bake in preheated oven 45 minutes or until set. Cool before removing from pan. Makes 8 to 10 servings.

———— EASTER CHEESECAKE ————

Crust:
**1 recipe Sweet Shortcrust Pastry,
  page 13**

Filling:
**8 oz. cream cheese, softened
1 cup cottage cheese, sieved
2/3 cup whipping cream
2 eggs
1/3 cup melted butter
Scant 1/2 cup sugar
Finely grated peel and juice of 1
  lemon
Pinch ground mace
1/3 cup currants**

Glaze:
1 egg yolk, beaten with pinch of salt

Garnish:
1/2 cup whipping cream

Preheat oven to 375F (190C). Grease a 9-inch springform pan. To prepare crust, on a lightly floured surface, roll Sweet Shortcrust Pastry to a 1/8-inch thickness. Line greased pan with dough. Prick dough with a fork. Refrigerate while preparing filling. Reserve leftover scraps of pastry for decoration. To prepare filling, beat cream cheese, cottage cheese, whipping cream, eggs, butter and sugar in a large bowl until smooth. Beat in lemon peel and juice and mace. Stir in currants. Spoon filling into prepared dough. Roll out pastry scraps and cut in 1/2-inch-wide strips. Lay strips over cheesecake in a criss-cross fashion. Brush with glaze of beaten egg yolk. Bake in preheated oven 40 minutes or until set. Whip cream until stiff. Garnish each serving with a dollop of whipped cream and serve warm. Makes 6 to 8 servings.

— STRAWBERRY CHEESE TARTS —

Crust:
1/3 cup butter
5-1/4 cups crushed cornflakes

Filling:
6 oz. cream cheese, softened
3/4 cup cottage cheese, sieved
2/3 cup sour cream
3 eggs, separated
Scant 1/2 cup sugar

Garnish:
18 small strawberries, sliced
18 sprigs fresh mint

To prepare crust, melt butter in a small saucepan over low heat. Stir in crushed cornflakes. Press mixture in 18 individual tartlet pans. Set aside. To prepare filling, beat cream cheese, cottage cheese, sour cream, egg yolks and 1/4 cup plus 2 tablespoons of sugar in a large bowl until smooth. Beat egg whites with remaining sugar until soft peaks form; fold into cheese mixture. Spoon filling into prepared crusts. Chill until set. To garnish, top each tart with a sliced strawberry and a sprig of mint. Makes 18 tarts.

—— BLACKBERRY INDIVIDUALS ——

6 tablespoons blackberry or
  blackcurrant preserves
4 oz. cream cheese, softened
1/2 cup cottage cheese, sieved
1/3 cup sour cream
Finely grated peel and juice of 1/2
  lemon
1 egg
3 tablespoons sugar

Garnish:
6 sprigs fresh mint

Preheat oven to 350F (175/C). Spread 1 tablespoon of blackcurrant preserves in each bottom of 6 ramekin dishes. Place dishes in a roasting pan. Set aside. Beat cream cheese, cottage cheese, sour cream, lemon peel and juice, egg and sugar in a medium-size bowl until smooth. Pour mixture into ramekin dishes. Add enough boiling water to roasting pan to reach half way up side of dishes. Bake in preheated oven 35 minutes or until just set. Remove from roasting pan and cool completely. To serve, run a knife around edge of cheesecakes and turn out on individual serving dishes. Garnish each cheesecake with a spring of mint. Makes 6 servings.

MANGO & RASPBERRY CHEESECAKE

Crust:
1/4 cup butter
1-3/4 cups graham cracker crumbs

Filling:
8 oz. cream cheese, softened
2/3 cup plain yogurt
2/3 cup sour cream
3 eggs, separated
Scant 1/2 cup sugar
1 tablespoon unflavored gelatin
2 tablespoons water
1-1/2 cups raspberries

Garnish:
1-1/2 cups raspberries
1 mango
2/3 cups whipping cream
8 to 10 sprigs fresh mint

Grease a 9-inch springform pan. To prepare crust, melt butter in a small saucepan over low heat. Stir in graham cracker crumbs. Press mixture in bottom of greased pan. Set aside. To prepare filling, beat cream cheese, yogurt, sour cream, egg yolks and 1/4 cup plus 2 tablespoons of sugar until smooth. Combine gelatin and water in a small saucepan. Simmer until gelatin is completely dissolved; stir into cheese mixture. Beat egg whites with remaining sugar until soft peaks form. Fold egg whites and raspberries into cheese mixture. Spoon filling into prepared crust. Refrigerate 2 to 3 hours or until set. To garnish, arrange raspberries in center of cheesecake in a mound. Peel and seed mango. Slice thinly and arrange in a fan pattern around raspberries. Whip cream until stiff. Pipe (with pastry bag) a border of 8 to 10 whipped cream rosettes around edge of cheesecake. Top each rosette with a sprig of mint. Makes 8 to 10 servings.

PUMPKIN CHEESECAKE

Crust:
**1 recipe Special Cheesecake Pastry,
page 12**

Filling:
1 lb. cream cheese, softened
3/4 cup sugar
2 eggs
1 (16-oz.) can pumpkin
1-1/2 teaspoons ground cinnamon
1 teaspoon ground allspice
1/4 teaspoon ground ginger
1/4 teaspoon ground mace

Garnish:
Toasted pumpkin seeds

Preheat oven to 350F (175C). Grease an 8-inch springform pan. To prepare crust, on a lightly floured surface, roll Special Cheesecake Pastry to a 1/4-inch thickness. Line bottom of greased pan with dough. Prick dough with a fork. Refrigerate while preparing filling. To prepare filling, beat cream cheese, sugar and eggs in a large bowl until smooth. Beat pumpkin and spices into cheese mixture until smooth. Spoon filling into prepared dough. Bake in preheated oven 45 minutes or until set. Cool completely before removing from pan. To garnish, arrange pumpkin seeds around edge of cheesecake. Makes 8 to 10 servings.

ICEBOX CHEESECAKE

Crust:
1/3 cup butter
1-3/4 cups crushed vanilla wafers
1/2 teaspoon ground ginger

Filling:
1 lb. cream cheese, softened
Finely grated peel and juice of 1
   lemon
4 eggs, separated
2/3 cup sugar
1 tablespoon plus 1 teaspoon
   unflavored gelatin
2 tablespoons water
1/4 cup whipping cream, whipped

Garnish:
1 (8-1/4-oz.) can pineapple rings,
   drained
Angelica pieces, cut in "leaves"
Maraschino cherries

Grease an 8-inch springform pan. To prepare crust, melt butter in a small saucepan over low heat. Stir in crushed vanilla wafers and ginger. Press mixture in bottom of greased pan. Set aside. To prepare filling, beat cream cheese, lemon peel and juice, egg yolks and 1/3 cup of sugar until smooth. Combine gelatin and water in a small saucepan. Simmer until gelatin is completely dissolved; stir into cheese mixture. Fold whipped cream into cheese mixture. Beat egg whites with remaining sugar until soft peaks form; fold into cheese mixture. Spoon filling into prepared crust. Freeze 3 to 4 hours. To garnish, cut pineapple rings in half and arrange around edge of cheesecake. Place angelica "leaves" and a cherry in center of every other ring. Makes 8 to 10 servings.

LINDY'S CHEESECAKE

Crust:
2 cups all-purpose flour
1/4 cup sugar
Finely grated peel of 1/2 lemon
2/3 cup firm butter, cut in small pieces
1 egg, beaten

Filling:
1-1/2 lb. cream cheese, softened
1 cup sour cream
2/3 cup sugar
2 tablespoons all-purpose flour
5 egg yolks
3 egg whites
Finely grated peel and juice of 1 orange
Finely grated peel and juice of 1 lemon
1/2 teaspoon vanilla extract

Garnish:
Powdered sugar
10 to 12 strawberries

To prepare crust, sift flour into a large bowl. Add sugar and lemon peel. Using 2 knives or a pastry blender, cut in butter until mixture resembles coarse bread crumbs. Add egg and work to form a smooth dough; do not overwork. Place dough in a plastic bag and refrigerate 30 minutes. Preheat oven to 475F (245C). Grease an 8-inch springform pan. On a lightly floured surface, roll dough to a 1/4-inch thickness. Line greased pan with dough. Set aside. To prepare filling, beat cream cheese, sour cream, sugar, flour and egg yolks and whites in a large bowl. Stir in citrus peel and juice and vanilla. Beat until smooth. Spoon filling into prepared crust. Bake in preheated oven 15 minutes. Adjust oven to 275F (135C). Bake 50 minutes more. Cool before removing from pan. To garnish, dust with powdered sugar. Place a strawberry on each serving. Makes 10 to 12 servings.

COFFEE & GOLDEN RAISIN CHEESECAKE

Filling:
1/3 cup golden raisins
1/4 cup coffee-flavored liqueur
12 oz. cream cheese, softened
2/3 cup whipping cream
3 eggs
1/4 cup all-purpose flour
2 tablespoons instant coffee granules
2 tablespoons boiling water

Crust:
1 recipe Special Cheesecake Pastry, page 12

Topping:
1/4 cup water
1 tablespoon sugar
3 oz. semisweet chocolate, broken in pieces
3 oz. cream cheese, softened

Garnish:
Chocolate candy coffee beans

To prepare filling, soak raisins in liqueur until plump. To speed process, boil raisins and liqueur in a small saucepan; cool. Preheat oven to 375F (190C). Grease a 9-inch springform pan. To prepare crust, on a lightly floured surface, roll Special Cheesecake Pastry to a 1/4-inch thickness. Line bottom of greased pan with dough. Prick dough with a fork. Refrigerate while preparing filling. Beat cream cheese, whipping cream, eggs and flour in a large bowl until smooth. Dissolve coffee granules in boiling water. Beat coffee into cheese mixture. Stir in raisins and liqueur. Spoon filling into prepared dough. Bake in preheated oven 50 minutes or until set. To prepare topping, in a small saucepan, bring water and sugar to a boil; remove from heat. Stir in chocolate and cool. Beat into cream cheese until smooth and creamy. Spread topping over cheesecake. Garnish with candy coffee beans. Makes 10 to 12 servings.

—— RASPBERRY CHEESE ROLL ——

Spongecake:
4 eggs
1/2 cup sugar
1/2 cup ground almonds
2 tablespoons all-purpose flour

Filling:
6 oz. cream cheese, sieved
2/3 cup whipping cream
1 tablespon powdered sugar
1 lb. raspberries

Garnish:
2/3 cup whipping cream
6 to 8 springs fresh mint

Preheat oven to 400F (205C). Grease a baking sheet and line with waxed paper. Beat eggs and sugar in a medium-size bowl until they are thick and foamy and hold a ribbon when drawn over surface. Sift ground almonds and flour over egg mixture and fold in. Spread mixture on prepared baking sheet. Bake in preheated oven 10 to 12 minutes or until springy to touch. Turn out on a wire rack and cool. In a blender or food processor, process cream cheese, whipping cream and powdered sugar until smooth. Do not overblend or whipping cream will separate. Peel waxed paper from spongecake. Spread cheese mixture on spongecake. Reserve 6 to 8 raspberries. Sprinkle remaining raspberries over cheese mixture. Roll spongecake up lightly, jelly-roll fashion. To garnish, whip cream until stiff. Pipe (with a pastry bag) 6 to 8 whipped cream rosettes along top of cheese roll. Place a reserved raspberry and a sprig of mint in each rosette. Makes 6 to 8 servings.

BOSTON CHEESECAKE

Crust:
1/4 cup butter
2 cups crushed vanilla wafers
1/4 teaspoon ground cinnamon
1/4 teaspoon ground allspice

Filling:
1 lb. cream cheese, softened
1 cup sour cream
2/3 cup sugar
4 eggs, separated
2 tablespoons all-purpose flour
1/2 teaspoon vanilla extract
Finely grated peel and juice of 1
    lemon

Garnish:
Powdered sugar

Preheat oven to 350F (175C). Grease a 9-inch springform pan. To prepare crust, melt butter in a small saucepan over low heat. Stir in crushed vanilla wafers and spices. Press mixture in bottom of greased pan. Set aside. To prepare filling, beat cream cheese, sour cream, 1/3 cup of sugar, egg yolks, flour, vanilla and lemon peel and juice in a large bowl until smooth. Beat egg whites with remaining sugar until soft peaks form; fold into cheese mixture. Spoon filling into prepared crust. Bake in preheated oven 1 hour or until set. Cool before removing from pan. To garnish, dust with powdered sugar. Makes 10 to 12 servings.

── STRAWBERRY SMOOTH CAKE ──

Crust:
**1 recipe Special Cheesecake Pastry,
  page 12**
2 tablespoons strawberry jam

Filling:
1 lb. cream cheese, softened
1 cup sour cream
4 eggs yolks
1/3 cup sugar
2 tablespoons all-purpose flour
**Finely grated peel and juice of 1
  orange**
3 egg whites

Topping:
2 pint baskets strawberries
**2 tablespoons red currant jelly, if
  desired**

Preheat oven to 325F (165C). Grease a 9-inch springform pan. To prepare crust, on a lightly floured surface, roll Special Cheesecake Pastry to a 1/4-inch thickness. Line bottom of greased pan with dough. Prick dough with a fork. Spread strawberry jam over dough. Refrigerate while preparing filling. To prepare filling, beat cream cheese, sour cream, egg yolks, 1/4 cup of sugar and orange peel and juice in a large bowl until smooth. Beat egg whites with remaining sugar until soft peaks form; fold into cheese mixture. Spoon filling into prepared crust. Bake in preheated oven on bottom rack 1 hour. Cool before removing from pan. To garnish, reserve 1 strawberry. Slice remaining strawberries. Arrange slices, pointed ends outwards, around edge of cheesecake. Repeat with more circles, overlapping layers slightly. If desired, melt jelly in a small saucepan. Brush strawberries with jelly. Makes 8 to 10 servings.

MANHATTAN CHEESECAKE

Crust:
1/4 cup butter
1-3/4 cups graham cracker crumbs

Filling:
8 oz. cream cheese, softened
2 cups cottage cheese, sieved
2 teaspoons vanilla extract
Pinch salt
3 eggs, separated
2/3 cup evaporated milk
2 tablespoons all-purpose flour
1 tablespoon lemon juice
2/3 cup sugar

Garnish:
Assorted fresh fruit
Sprigs fresh mint

Preheat oven to 350F (175C). Grease a 9-inch springform pan. To prepare crust, melt butter in a small saucepan over low heat. Stir in graham cracker crumbs. Press mixture in bottom of greased pan. Set aside. To prepare filling, beat cream cheese, cottage cheese, vanilla, salt, egg yolks, milk, flour and lemon juice in a large bowl until smooth. Beat egg whites with sugar until soft peaks form; fold into cheese mixture. Spoon filling into prepared crust. Bake in preheated oven 1 hour or until set. Chill cheesecake. To garnish, slice fruit and arrange on cheesecake. Top with sprigs of mint. Makes 10 to 12 servings.

TROPICAL CHEESECAKE

Crust:
1 recipe Plain Spongecake Border,
   page 10
1/4 cup butter
1-3/4 cups crushed gingersnaps

Filling:
8 oz. cream cheese, softened
1 cup plain yogurt
2 eggs, separated
1/2 cup sugar
1 tablespoon unflavored gelatin
2 tablespoons water
2/3 cup whipping cream, whipped

Garnish:
1 lb. assorted fresh fruit

Grease bottom of a 9-inch spring-form pan. To prepare crust, cut Plain Spongecake Border to same height as greased pan; wrap strips around sides of pan. Melt butter in a small saucepan over low heat. Stir in crushed gingersnaps. Press mixture in bottom of prepared pan. Set aside. To prepare filling, beat cream cheese, yogurt, egg yolks and 1/4 cup plus 2 tablespoons of sugar until smooth. Combine gelatin and water in a small saucepan. Simmer until gelatin is completely dissolved; stir into cheese mixture. Fold whipped cream into cheese mixture. Beat egg whites with remaining sugar until soft peaks form; fold into cheese mixture. Spoon filling into prepared crust. Refrigerate 2 to 3 hours or until set. To garnish, cut fruit in even-sized pieces; arrange on cheesecake. Makes 8 to 10 servings.

—— STRAWBERRY CHEESE FLAN ——

Crust:
**1 recipe Special Cheesecake Pastry,
page 12**

Filling:
**6 oz. cream cheese, softened
Finely grated peel and juice of 1
     orange
1/2 teaspoon vanilla extract
3 egg yolks
1/4 cup sugar
2/3 cup whipping cream**

Topping:
**2 pint baskets strawberries, hulled
1/4 cup strawberry jam
1 tablespoon water**

Grease a 9-inch flan mold. To prepare crust, on a lightly floured surface, roll Special Cheesecake Pastry
to a 1/4-inch thickness. Line greased
mold with dough. Refrigerate 30
minutes. Preheat oven to 400F
(205C). Fill dough with dried beans
or dried pasta. Bake in preheated
oven 35 minutes or until lightly
browned. Set aside. To prepare filling, beat cream cheese, orange peel
and juice and vanilla until smooth. In
a small bowl, beat egg yolks and sugar
until pale in color. Bring whipping
cream to a simmer in a medium-size
saucepan. Gradually beat egg yolk
mixture into whipping cream. Continue stirring until mixture thickens.
Cool and beat into cheese mixture.
Spoon filling into prepared crust. Refrigerate 2 to 3 hours or until set. To
garnish, arrange strawberries over
filling so strawberries are standing
up. Heat jam and water in a small
saucepan until liquified; brush over
strawberries. Makes 6 servings.

APRICOT & ALMOND CHEESECAKE

Crust:
1/3 cup butter
1-3/4 cups graham cracker crumbs

Filling:
8 oz. Neufchâtel cheese, softened
2/3 cup plain yogurt
3/4 cup ground almonds
1/2 cup sugar
2/3 cup whipping cream, whipped
1 tablespoon unflavored gelatin
2 tablespoons water
2 eggs
1/2 teaspoon almond extract

Garnish:
1 (16-oz.) can apricot halves, drained
2/3 cup whipping cream

Grease an 8-inch-square baking pan. To prepare crust, melt butter in a small saucepan over low heat. Stir in graham cracker crumbs. Press mixture in bottom of greased pan. Set aside. To prepare filling, beat Neufchâtel cheese, yogurt, almonds and 1/4 cup of sugar in a large bowl until smooth. Fold whipped cream into cheese mixture. Combine gelatin with water. Simmer until gelatin is completely dissolved; stir into cheese mixture. Beat eggs, remaining sugar and almond extract until they are thick and foamy and hold a ribbon when drawn over surface; fold into cheese mixture. Spoon filling into prepared crust. Refrigerate 2 to 3 hours or until set. Cut cheesecake in 2-inch squares. To garnish, place 1 apricot half in center of each square. Whip cream until stiff. Pipe (with a pastry bag) a border of whipped cream around edge of each square. Makes 16 servings.

—— BLUEBERRY CHEESECAKE ——

Crust:
1/2 cup butter
1-3/4 cups graham cracker crumbs
2 tablespoons cream sherry

Filling:
12 oz. ricotta cheese
1/3 cup plain yogurt
Scant 1/2 cup sugar
1 tablespoon lemon juice
2 eggs, separated
1 lb. blueberries
1 tablespoon unflavored gelatin
2 tablespoons water

Topping:
1/4 cup red currant jelly
2/3 cup whipping cream, whipped

Garnish:
8 to 10 sprigs fresh mint

Grease a 9-inch springform pan. To prepare crust, melt butter in a small saucepan over low heat. Stir in graham cracker crumbs and cream sherry. Press mixture in bottom of greased pan. Refrigerate while preparing filling. To prepare filling, beat ricotta cheese, yogurt, 1/4 cup plus 2 tablespoons of sugar, lemon juice and egg yolks in a medium-size bowl. Add 1/4 of blueberries and stir gently. Combine gelatin and water in a small saucepan. Simmer until gelatin is completely dissolved; stir into cheese mixture. Beat egg whites with remaining sugar until soft peaks form; fold into cheese mixture. Spoon filling into prepared crust. Refrigerate 2 to 3 hours or until set. To prepare topping, heat red currant jelly in a small saucepan until liquified. Stir in remaining blueberries. Spoon on cheesecake and chill. Garnish each serving with a sprig of mint. Makes 8 to 10 servings.

COEURS À LA CRÈME

8 oz. cream cheese, softened
2 cups cottage cheese, sieved
1 teaspoon vanilla extract, if desired
2/3 cup whipping cream

Garnish:
6 strawberries, sliced

Lightly grease 6 individual coeur à la crème molds or 1 large mold. Beat cream cheese in a medium-size bowl until fluffy. Beat in cottage cheese until mixture is smooth. Stir in vanilla, if desired. Spoon cheese mixture into prepared molds. Refrigerate until set. Turn out onto individual plates. Whip cream until stiff. Spread whipped cream over Coeurs à La Creme. Garnish with strawberry slices. Makes 6 servings.

—— PASSION FRUIT CHEESECAKE ——

Crust:
1/4 cup butter
1-3/4 cups graham cracker crumbs

Filling:
8 oz. cream cheese, softened
1 cup plain yogurt
2 eggs, separated
Scant 1/2 cup sugar
5 passion fruit
Juice of 1 lemon
1 tablespoon plus 1 teaspoon
  unflavored gelatin
2 tablespoons water

Topping:
5 passion fruit
1/4 cup orange juice
1 tablespoon plus 2 teaspoons sugar
2 tablespoons cornstarch
3 tablespoons water

Grease a 9-inch springform pan. To prepare crust, melt butter in a small saucepan over low heat. Stir in graham cracker crumbs. Press mixture in bottom of greased pan. Set aside. To prepare filling, beat cream cheese, yogurt, egg yolks and 1/4 cup of sugar in a large bowl until smooth. Cut passion fruit in half. Scoop flesh and seeds into a blender or a food processor. Process until seeds have come away from flesh. Strain juice into a saucepan; discard seeds. Add lemon juice and 1 tablespoon plus 2 teaspoons of sugar. Bring to a boil and remove from heat. Combine gelatin and water in a small saucepan. Simmer until gelatin is completely dissolved; stir into juice. Cool juice to room temperature; stir into cheese mixture. Beat egg whites with remaining sugar until soft peaks form; fold into cheese mixture. Spoon filling into prepared crust. Refrigerate 2 to 3 hours or until set. To prepare topping, cut passion fruit in half. Scoop flesh and seeds into a stainless steel saucepan. Stir in orange juice and sugar and bring to a boil. Combine cornstarch and water; add to passion fruit. Simmer until thickened. Cool to room temperature and pour on cheesecake. Refrigerate until topping is set. Makes 8 to 10 servings.

———— POLKA DOT CHEESECAKE ————

Crust:
1 recipe Plain Spongecake Border,
   page 10
1/3 cup butter
1-3/4 cups crushed vanilla wafers

Filling:
8 oz. ricotta cheese
2/3 cup sour cream
Scant 1/2 cup sugar
3 egg yolks
1 tablespoon unflavored gelatin
2 tablespoons water
2/3 cup whipping cream, whipped

Topping:
3 egg whites
1/4 cup sugar
8 oz. red currants or raspberries
Additional sugar

Grease a 9-inch springform pan. To prepare crust, cut Plain Spongecake Border so that it reaches 1/2 inch above top of greased pan; wrap strips around sides of pan. Melt butter in a small saucepan over low heat. Stir in crushed vanilla wafers. Press mixture in prepared pan. Set aside. To prepare filling, beat ricotta cheese, sour cream, sugar and egg yolks in a large bowl until smooth. Combine gelatin and water in a small saucepan. Simmer until gelatin is completely dissolved; beat into cheese mixture. Fold whipped cream into cheese mixture. Spoon filling into prepared crust. Refrigerate 2 to 3 hours or until set. To prepare topping, beat egg whites with sugar until soft peaks form. Fold currants or raspberries into egg whites. Mound on cheesecake. Dust with additional sugar. Broil until golden brown. Makes 6 to 8 servings.

—— POMEGRANATE CHEESECAKE ——

Crust:
1/3 cup butter
1-3/4 cups crushed gingersnaps

Filling:
12 oz. ricotta cheese
2/3 cup plain yogurt
2 eggs, separated -
Scant 1/2 cup sugar
Pinch of ground cloves
1 small pomegranate
Finely grated peel and juice of 2
   oranges
1 tablespoon unflavored gelatin

Topping:
1/3 cup grenadine syrup
2 tablespoons orange juice
2 tablespoons cornstarch
3 tablespoons water
1 small pomegranate

Garnish:
2/3 cup whipping cream
1 orange, sliced

To prepare crust, melt butter. Stir in crushed gingersnaps. Press mixture in a greased 9-inch springform pan. To prepare filling, beat ricotta cheese, yogurt, egg yolks, 1/4 cup plus 2 tablespoons of sugar and cloves until smooth. Cut pomegranate in half; remove seeds. Stir seeds into cheese mixture. Combine orange peel and juice and gelatin. Simmer until gelatin is completely dissolved; stir into cheese mixture. Beat egg whites with remaining sugar until soft peaks form; fold into cheese mixture. Spoon filling into crust. Refrigerate 2 to 3 hours or until set. To prepare topping, bring grenadine syrup and orange juice to a boil. Combine cornstarch and water; stir into syrup mixture. Simmer until thickened. Cut pomegranate in half; remove seeds. Stir seeds into topping. Cool to room temperature; pour over cheesecake. Refrigerate until set. To garnish, whip cream until stiff. Pipe (with a pastry bag) a border of small rosettes around edge of cheesecake. Decorate with orange slices. Makes 8 to 10 servings.

—— REFRIGERATOR CHEESECAKE ——

Crust:
1/3 cup butter
1-3/4 cups crushed vanilla wafers

Filling:
12 oz. cream cheese, softened
2/3 cup sour cream
2/3 cup plain yogurt
Scant 1/2 cup sugar
3 eggs, separated
**1 tablespoon plus 1 teaspoon
   unflavored gelatin**
2 tablespoons water
2/3 cup whipping cream, whipped

Garnish:
1 lb. assorted fresh fruit

Grease an 8-inch springform pan. To prepare crust, melt butter in a small saucepan over low heat. Stir in crushed vanilla wafers. Press mixture in greased pan. Set aside. To prepare filling, beat cream cheese, sour cream, yogurt, 1/4 cup plus 2 table-spoons of sugar and egg yolks in a large bowl until smooth. Combine gelatin and water in a small saucepan. Simmer until gelatin is completely dissolved; stir into cheese mixture. Fold whipped cream into cheese mix-ture. Beat egg whites with remaining sugar until soft peaks form; fold into cheese mixture. Spoon filling into prepared crust. Refrigerate 2 to 3 hours or until set. To garnish, cut fruit in even-sized pieces; arrange on cheesecake. Makes 8 to 10 servings.

—— LEMON MERINGUE POSSET ——

Crust:
1/2 cup butter
2-1/2 cups graham cracker crumbs

Filling:
3 egg yolks
1 cup whipping cream
Juice of 2 lemons
Scant 1/2 cup sugar

Topping:
3 egg whites
1 tablespoon plus 2 teaspoons sugar
Additional sugar

Garnish:
8 to 10 lemon peel twists
8 to 10 sprigs fresh mint

Grease an 8-inch flan mold. To prepare crust, melt butter in a small saucepan over low heat. Stir in graham cracker crumbs. Press mixture in greased mold. Set aside. To prepare filling, beat egg yolks until pale in color. Bring cream to a boil in a small saucepan. Stir in lemon juice and sugar. Beat hot cream mixture into egg yolks. Spoon filling into prepared crust. Refrigerate 2 to 3 hours or until set. To prepare topping, beat egg whites with 1 tablespoon plus 2 teaspoons sugar until soft peaks form. Mound on flan. Sprinkle with additional sugar. Broil until golden brown. Garnish each serving with a twist of lemon peel and a sprig of mint. Makes 8 to 10 servings.

— MARSHMALLOW CHEESECAKE —

Crust:
1/3 cup butter
1-3/4 cups crushed zwieback toast

Filling:
12 oz. pink and white marshmallows,
** cut in small pieces**
1/3 cup milk
1 lb. Neufchâtel cheese, softened
2 tablespoons lemon juice
1 cup whipping cream, whipped
2 to 3 drops pink food coloring

Garnish:
12 pink and white marshmallows
2 oz. semisweet chocolate, melted

Grease a 9-inch springform pan. To prepare crust, melt butter in a small saucepan over low heat. Stir in crushed zwieback toast. Press mixture in greased pan. Set aside. To prepare filling, combine marshmallows and milk in large saucepan over low heat. Stir occasionally until marshmallows melt; cool. Beat Neufchâtel cheese and lemon juice in a large bowl. Blend in marshmallow mixture until smooth. Fold in whipped cream. Add food coloring until desired pink shade is reached. Spoon filling into prepared crust. Refrigerate 2 to 3 hours or until set. To garnish, cut marshmallows in half. Arrange a border of pink and white marshmallows around edge of cheesecake. Melt chocolate in top of a double boiler or a bowl set over a pan of simmering water. Drizzle melted chocolate in center of cheesecake. Makes 8 to 10 servings.

INDIVIDUAL
STRAWBERRY CHEESECAKES

Crust:
1/4 cup butter
1-1/4 cups graham cracker crumbs

Filling:
8 oz. cream cheese, softened
1-1/4 cups plain yogurt
2 egg yolks
Scant 1/2 cup sugar
1 tablespoon unflavored gelatin
2 tablespoons water

Garnish:
2 pint baskets strawberries, hulled
2/3 cup whipped cream
10 sprigs fresh mint

Grease 10 muffin cups. To prepare crust, melt butter in a small saucepan over low heat. Stir in graham cracker crumbs. Press mixture in bottoms of greased muffin cups. Set aside. To prepare filling, beat cream cheese, yogurt, egg yolks and sugar in a large bowl until smooth. Combine gelatin with water in a small saucepan. Simmer until gelatin is completely dissolved; stir into cheese mixture. Spoon filling into prepared crusts. Refrigerate 2 to 3 hours or until set. Remove cheesecakes from muffin cups. To garnish, slice strawberries and arrange on cheesecakes. Whip cream until stiff. Pipe (with a pastry bag) a whipped cream rosette on each cheesecake. Top rosettes with sprigs of mint. Makes 10 cheesecakes.

——BLACK CHERRY CHEESECAKE——

Crust:
1/4 cup butter
1-3/4 cups graham cracker crumbs

Filling:
1 lb. Neufchâtel cheese, softened
2/3 cup plain yogurt
1/4 cup sugar
Grated peel and juice of 1 lemon
4 teaspoons unflavored gelatin
2 tablespoons water
1 egg white

Topping:
2 tablespoons black cherry jam
1 (16-1/2-oz.) can black cherries,
  drained, pitted

Garnish:
6 to 8 sprigs fresh mint

Grease an 8" x 4" loaf pan and line with waxed paper. To prepare crust, melt butter in a small saucepan over low heat. Stir in graham cracker crumbs. Press mixture in bottom of prepared pan. Set aside. To prepare filling, beat Neufchâtel cheese, yogurt, 1 tablespoon plus 1 teaspoon of sugar and lemon peel and juice in a large bowl until light and smooth. Combine gelatin and water in a saucepan. Simmer until gelatin is completely dissolved; stir into cheese mixture. Beat egg white with remaining sugar until soft peaks form; fold into cheese mixture. Spoon filling into prepared crust. Refrigerate 2 to 3 hours or until set. To prepare topping, heat black cherry jam in a small saucepan until liquified. Add cherries and spread on cheesecake. Refrigerate until set. Garnish each serving with a sprig of mint. Makes 6 to 8 servings.

PEACH & RASPBERRY CHEESECAKE

Crust:
1/3 cup butter
1-3/4 cups crushed gingersnaps

Filling:
4 oz. cream cheese, softened
1/2 cup plain yogurt
1/3 cup sugar
2/3 cup whipping cream, whipped
1 tablespoon plus 1 teaspoon
    unflavored gelatin
2 tablespoons water
1 (14-oz.) can sliced peaches, drained,
    coarsely chopped
2 eggs

Garnish:
12 oz. raspberries
2/3 cup whipping cream
1/2 cup toasted slivered almonds

Grease a 9-inch springform pan. To prepare crust, melt butter in a small saucepan over low heat. Stir in crushed gingersnaps. Press mixture in bottom of greased pan. Refrigerate while preparing filling. To prepare filling, beat cream cheese, yogurt and 1 tablespoon plus 2 teaspoons of sugar in a large bowl until smooth. Fold in whipped cream. Combine gelatin and water in a small saucepan. Simmer until gelatin is completely dissolved; stir into cheese mixture. Stir in peaches. Beat eggs and remaining sugar until they are thick and foamy and hold a ribbon when drawn across surface; fold into cheese mixture. Spoon filling into prepared crust. Refrigerate 2 to 3 hours or until set. To garnish, arrange raspberries on cheesecake leaving a 1-inch border around edge. Whip cream until stiff. Pipe (with a pastry bag) a border of whipped cream rosettes around edge of cheesecake. Place almonds in each rosette. Makes 10 servings.

——BLACKBERRY CHEESECAKE——

Crust:
1/4 cup butter
1-3/4 cups graham cracker crumbs

Filling:
1 lb. ricotta cheese
1/3 cup plus 1 tablespoon sugar
2 tablespoons lemon juice
2 eggs, separated
14 oz. blackberries

Topping:
2/3 cup blackberry-flavored fruit juice
2 tablespoons cornstarch
1/4 cup water

Preheat oven to 375F (190C). Grease a 9-inch springform pan. To prepare crust, melt butter in a small saucepan over low heat. Stir in graham cracker crumbs. Press mixture in greased pan. Set aside. To prepare filling, beat ricotta cheese, 1/3 cup of sugar, lemon juice and egg yolks in a large bowl until smooth. Stir in 1/3 of blackberries. Beat egg whites with remaining sugar until soft peaks form; fold into cheese mixture. Spoon filling into prepared crust. Bake in preheated oven 40 minutes or until set. To prepare topping, bring juice to a boil in small saucepan. Combine cornstarch and water; stir into juice. Simmer until thickened. Stir in remaining blackberries. Spread on cheesecake. Cool before removing from pan. Makes 8 to 10 servings.

———— PINEAPPLE CHEESECAKE ————

Crust:
1/4 cup butter
1-3/4 cups graham cracker crumbs
Pinch of ground cinnamon

Filling:
12 oz. cream cheese, softened
2 eggs
1/2 cup sugar
2 teaspoons all-purpose flour
1/2 teaspoon vanilla extract

Garnish:
1 (3-1/4-oz.) can pineapple rings,
  drained, cut in pieces
Maraschino cherries
Fresh pineapple leaves
1/4 cup apricot jam
1 tablespoon water

Preheat oven to 350F (175C). Grease a 9-inch springform pan. To prepare crust, melt butter in a small saucepan over low heat. Stir in graham cracker crumbs and cinnamon. Press mixture in greased pan. Set aside. To prepare filling, beat cream cheese, eggs, sugar, flour and vanilla in a large bowl until smooth. Spoon filling into prepared crust. Bake in preheated oven 45 minutes or until set. Cool before removing from pan. Garnish with pineapple pieces, cherries and pineapple leaves. Heat apricot jam and water in a small saucepan until jam liquifies; brush over fruit. Makes 8 servings.

—— STRAWBERRY CHEESECAKE ——

Crust:
1/3 cup butter
1-3/4 cups crushed vanilla wafers

Filling:
8 oz. ricotta cheese
2/3 cup plain yogurt
2/3 cup sour cream
2 eggs, separated
Finely grated peel and juice of 1
  orange
2 pint baskets strawberries, hulled
1 tablespoon plus 2 teaspoons
  unflavored gelatin
2 tablespoons water
1/4 cup sugar

Garnish:
2/3 cup whipping cream

Grease a 9-inch springform pan. To prepare crust, melt butter in a small saucepan over low heat. Stir in crushed vanilla wafers. Press mixture in bottom of greased pan. Set aside. To prepare filling, beat ricotta cheese, yogurt, sour cream, egg yolks and orange peel and juice in a large bowl until smooth. Reserve 10 strawberries. Process remaining strawberries in a food processor or blender 30 seconds or until pureed. Stir into cheese mixture. Combine gelatin with water in a small saucepan. Simmer until gelatin is completely dissolved; stir into cheese mixture. Beat egg whites with sugar until soft peaks form; fold into cheese mixture. Spoon filling into prepared crust. Refrigerate 2 to 3 hours or until set. To garnish, whip cream until stiff. Pipe (with a pastry bag) a border of 20 whipped cream rosettes around edge of cheesecake. Cut reserved strawberries in half. Top each rosette with a strawberry half. Makes 8 to 10 servings.

MANDARIN ORANGE CHEESECAKE

Crust:
1/3 cup butter
1-2/3 cups crushed zwieback toast
1/4 cup sugar

Filling:
12 oz. cream cheese, softened
1-1/2 cups cottage cheese, sieved
Finely grated peel and juice of 1
  orange
2 eggs
1/4 cup sugar

Garnish:
1 (16-oz.) can mandarin oranges,
  drained
1/4 cup strained apricot preserves
Fresh mint leaves

Preheat oven to 375F (190C). Grease a 9-inch springform pan. To prepare crust, melt butter in a saucepan over low heat. Stir in crushed zwieback toast and sugar. Press mixture in greased pan. Set aside. To prepare filling, beat cream cheese, cottage cheese, orange peel and juice, eggs and sugar until smooth. Spoon filling into prepared crust. Bake in preheated oven 40 minutes or until set. Cool before removing from pan. To garnish, arrange orange segments around edge of cheesecake. Heat preserves in a small saucepan until liquified. Brush over oranges. Decorate with mint leaves. Makes 8 to 10 servings.

—— RASPBERRY CHEESECAKE ——

Crust:
1 recipe Chocolate Stripe Spongecake Border, page 11
1/4 cup butter
1-3/4 cups graham cracker crumbs

Filling:
8 oz. cream cheese, softened
2/3 cup plain yogurt
2/3 cup sour cream
2 eggs, separated
1/3 cup sugar
1 tablespoon unflavored gelatin
2 tablespoons water

Garnish:
1 lb. raspberries
2/3 cup whipping cream
1 packet round plain chocolate candy wafers

Grease bottom of a 9-inch spring-form pan. To prepare crust, cut Chocolate Stripe Spongecake Border to fit 3 inches up sides of greased pan; wrap strips around sides of pan. Melt butter in a small saucepan over low heat. Stir in graham cracker crumbs. Press mixture in bottom of greased pan. To prepare filling, beat cream cheese, yogurt, sour cream, egg yolks and 1/4 cup of sugar in a large bowl until smooth. Combine gelatin and water in a small saucepan. Simmer until gelatin is completely dissolved; stir into cheese mixture. Beat egg whites with remaining sugar until soft peaks form; fold into cheese mixture. Spoon filling into prepared crust. Refrigerate 2 to 3 hours or until set. When cheesecake has set, trim spongecake border to 1/2 inch above surface of cheesecake. To garnish, arrange raspberries on cheesecake. Whip cream until stiff. Pipe (with a pastry bag) a border of whipped cream rosettes around edge of cheesecake. Place raspberries and chocolate candy wafers on alternate rosettes. Makes 8 to 10 servings.

—— GOOSEBERRY CHEESECAKE ——

Crust:
1/3 cup butter
1-1/4 cups graham cracker crumbs
3 tablespoons sunflower kernels

Filling:
12 oz. cream cheese, softened
1-1/2 cups cottage cheese, sieved
Juice of 1 lemon
1 teaspoon orange flower water
2 eggs
1/4 cup sugar

Topping:
1 (16-1/2-oz.) can gooseberries
2 tablespoons cornstarch
1/4 cup water

Preheat oven to 375F (190C). Grease a 9-inch springform pan. To prepare crust, melt butter in a small saucepan over low heat. Stir in graham cracker crumbs and sunflower kernels. Press mixture in greased pan. Set aside. To prepare filling, beat cream cheese, cottage cheese, lemon juice, orange flower water, eggs and sugar in a medium-size bowl until smooth. Spoon filling into prepared crust. Bake in preheated oven 40 minutes or until set. To prepare topping, drain juice from gooseberries into a small saucepan. Bring to a boil. Combine cornstarch and water; stir into juice. Simmer until thickened. Stir in gooseberries and spread on cheesecake. Cool before removing from pan. Makes 8 to 10 servings.

LEMON CHEESECAKE

Crust:
1/3 cup butter
1-3/4 cups graham cracker crumbs
Pinch of ground mace

Filling:
8 oz. cream cheese, softened
1 cup plain yogurt
2 eggs, separated
1/2 cup sugar
Finely grated peel and juice of 2
lemons
1 tablespoon plus 1 teaspoon
unflavored gelatin
2 tablespoons water

Topping:
1/2 cup water
2 drops yellow food coloring
2 tablespoons sugar
2 teaspoons cornstarch
1 tablespoon water

Garnish:
Marzipan "lemons"
Angelica pieces, cut in strips
2/3 cup whipping cream

To prepare crust, melt butter over low heat. Stir in graham cracker crumbs and mace. Press mixture in bottom of a greased 9-inch spring-form pan and refrigerate. To prepare filling, beat cream cheese, yogurt, egg yolks, 1/4 cup of sugar and lemon peel and juice until smooth. Combine gelatin and water in a small saucepan. Simmer until gelatin is completely dissolved; stir into cheese mixture. Beat egg whites with remaining sugar until stiff peaks form; fold into cheese mixture. Spoon filling into prepared crust. Refrigerate 2 to 3 hours or until set. To prepare topping, bring 1/2 cup water, food coloring and sugar to a boil. Combine cornstarch with 1 tablespoon water; stir into sugar water. Simmer until thickened. Cool slightly and pour over cheesecake. Refrigerate until topping is set. To garnish, whip cream until stiff. Pipe (with a pastry bag) a border of whipped cream rosettes around edge of cheesecake. Place "lemons" and angelica strips on alternate rosettes. Makes 8 to 10 servings.

—— CRANBERRY CHEESECAKE ——

Crust:
1/4 cup butter
1-3/4 cups graham cracker crumbs

Filling:
12 oz. cranberries
2/3 cup sugar
Boiling water
6 oz. cream cheese, softened
2 eggs, separated
1 tablespoon unflavored gelatin
2 tablespoons water
Finely grated peel and juice of 1
orange
2/3 cup whipping cream, whipped

Garnish:
2/3 cup whipping cream

Grease a 9-inch springform pan. To prepare crust, melt butter in a small saucepan over low heat. Stir in graham cracker crumbs. Press mixture in pan. Set aside. To prepare filling, combine cranberries and 1/4 cup of sugar in a medium-size saucepan. Cover berries with boiling water. Let stand 15 minutes or until slightly cooked. Beat cream cheese, remaining sugar and egg yolks in a medium-size bowl until smooth. Combine gelatin and water in a small saucepan. Simmer until gelatin is completely dissolved; stir into cheese mixture. Stir in 1/3 of cooked cranberries. Fold whipped cream into cheese mixture. Beat egg whites until soft peaks form; fold into cheese mixture. Spoon filling into prepared crust. Refrigerate 2 to 3 hours or until set. To garnish, whip cream until stiff. Pipe (with a pastry bag) a border of whipped cream rosettes around edge of cheesecake. Arrange remaining cooked cranberries in center. Makes 8 to 10 servings.

—— RED CURRANT CHEESECAKE ——

Crust:
1/4 cup butter
1-3/4 cups graham cracker crumbs

Filling:
12 oz. cream cheese, softened
1-1/2 cups cottage cheese, sieved
Finely grated peel and juice of 1
  lemon
2 eggs
1/4 cup sugar
12 oz. red currants

Topping:
1/4 cup red currant jelly

Garnish:
8 to 10 sprigs fresh mint

Preheat oven to 375F (190C). Grease a 9-inch springform pan. To prepare crust, melt butter in a small saucepan over low heat. Stir in graham cracker crumbs. Press mixture in bottom of greased pan. Set aside. To prepare filling, beat cream cheese, cottage cheese, lemon peel and juice, eggs and sugar in a large bowl until smooth. Stir in 1/3 of red currants. Spoon filling into prepared crust. Bake in preheated oven 45 minutes or until set. To prepare topping, heat red currant jelly in a small saucepan until liquified. Add remaining red currants. Spread on cheesecake. Cool before removing from pan. Garnish each serving with a sprig of mint. Makes 8 to 10 servings.

—— FIG & WALNUT CHEESECAKE ——

Filling:
3/4 cup dried figs, stems removed
Water
1 lb. ricotta cheese
2/3 cup whipping cream
2 eggs
2 tablespoons light-brown sugar
1 tablespoon all-purpose flour

Crust:
1/4 cup butter
1-1/4 cups graham cracker crumbs
1/2 cup ground walnuts

Garnish:
2 fresh figs
1 cup walnut halves

To prepare filling, cover figs with water in a saucepan. Bring to boil. Reduce heat, cover and simmer 15 minutes. Remove from heat and cool. Preheat oven to 325F (165C). Grease an 8-inch springform pan. To prepare crust, melt butter in a small saucepan over low heat. Stir in graham cracker crumbs and walnuts. Press mixture in greased pan. Set aside. Beat ricotta cheese, whipping cream, eggs and brown sugar in a large bowl until smooth. Coarsely chop figs. Stir figs and flour into cheese mixture. Spoon filling into prepared crust. Bake in preheated oven 1 hour and 10 minutes or until set. Cool before removing from pan. To garnish, trim tops from fresh figs; cut in slices. Arrange fig slices around edge of cheesecake. Place walnuts in center. Makes 8 to 10 servings.

MAIDS OF HONOR

Crust:
**1 recipe Sweet Shortcrust Pastry,
page 13**

Filling:
**6 oz. cream cheese, softened
3/4 cup cottage cheese, sieved
3 egg yolks
1/2 cup ground almonds
1/4 cup sugar
3 tablespoons milk
2 tablespoons currants
3 tablespoons apricot preserves
Freshly grated nutmeg**

Preheat oven to 375F (190C). Grease 24 tartlet pans. To prepare crust, on a lightly floured surface, roll Sweet Shortcrust Pastry, half at a time, as thinly as possible. Cut 24 circles 1-1/2 inches larger than tartlet pans. Press circles in greased pans; prick with a fork. Refrigerate while preparing filling. To prepare filling, beat cream cheese, cottage cheese, egg yolks, almonds and sugar in a large bowl until smooth. Add milk, a little at a time. Stir in currants. Spread 1/4 teaspoon of apricot preserves in bottom of each prepared pan; spoon in filling. Sprinkle with nutmeg. Bake in preheated oven 35 minutes or until golden brown. Makes 24 tarts.

—— GOLDEN RAISIN CURD CAKE ——

Crust:
1 recipe Sweet Shortcrust Pastry,
  page 13

Filling:
8 oz. cream cheese, softened
1 cup cottage cheese, sieved
1-1/4 cups sour cream
2 eggs
1/3 cup packed light-brown sugar
1/3 cup golden raisins
1 tablespoon self-rising flour

Topping:
3 cups lightly crushed cornflakes

Preheat oven to 350F (175C). Grease an 8-inch springform pan. To prepare crust, on a lightly floured surface, roll Sweet Shortcrust Pastry to a 1/4-inch thickness. Line bottom and 2 inches up sides of greased pan with dough. Refrigerate while preparing filling. To prepare filling, beat cream cheese, cottage cheese, sour cream, eggs and brown sugar in a large bowl until smooth. Stir raisins into flour to evenly coat; stir into cheese mixture. Spoon filling into prepared crust. Sprinkle with cornflakes. Bake in preheated oven 45 minutes or until set. Cool before removing from pan. Makes 8 to 10 servings.

─ PRUNE & WALNUT CHEESECAKE ─

Crust:
1/4 cup butter
1-1/2 cups crushed vanilla wafers
1/4 cup ground walnuts

Filling:
1 lb. ricotta cheese
2/3 cup sour cream
2 eggs
1/4 cup packed light-brown sugar
1 (16-oz.) can prunes, drained, pitted
3/4 cup chopped walnuts
1 tablespoon all-purpose flour

Garnish:
10 dried pitted prunes
3 oz. cream cheese, softened
2 tablespoons milk
2 tablespoons powdered sugar
1 tablespoon honey
3/4 cup finely chopped walnuts

Preheat oven to 325F (165C). Grease an 8-inch springform pan. To prepare crust, melt butter in a small saucepan over low heat. Stir in crushed vanilla wafers and walnuts. Press mixture in greased pan. Set aside. To prepare filling, beat ricotta cheese, sour cream, eggs and brown sugar in a large bowl until smooth. In a blender or food processor, process prunes to a puree. Stir prune puree, walnuts and flour into cheese mixture. Spoon filling into prepared crust. Bake in preheated oven 50 minutes or until set. Cool before removing from pan. To garnish, place prunes in a small saucepan; cover with water. Simmer 15 minutes, drain and cool. Beat cream cheese and milk to form a mixture of piping consistency. Stir in powdered sugar. Pipe (with a pastry bag) a border of cream cheese rosettes around edge of cheesecake. Stir honey into walnuts to form a paste. Stuff cooked prunes with walnut paste. Place a stuffed prune on each rosette. Makes 8 to 10 servings.

POPPY SEED CHEESECAKE

Crust:
1/4 cup butter
1 tablespoon honey
1 cup bulgur wheat

Filling:
1 lb. ricotta cheese
1/4 cup whipping cream
3 egg yolks
1 tablespoon all-purpose flour
1 tablespoon ground cinnamon
2 tablespoons poppyseeds
3 tablespoons honey

Topping:
1/4 cup butter
3/4 cup poppy seeds
2 tablespoons sugar
1 tablespoon all-purpose flour

Preheat oven to 350F (175C). Grease an 8-inch springform pan. To prepare crust, melt butter in a small saucepan over low heat. Stir in honey and bulgur wheat. Press mixture in greased pan. Set aside. To prepare filling, beat ricotta cheese, whipping cream, egg yolks, flour, cinnamon, poppyseeds and honey in a large bowl until smooth. Spoon filling into prepared crust. Bake in preheated oven 30 minutes. To prepare topping, melt butter in a small saucepan. Stir in poppyseeds, sugar and flour. Spread on partially-baked cheesecake. Bake 25 minutes more or until set. Cool before removing from pan. Makes 6 to 8 servings.

— COFFEE & WALNUT CHEESECAKE —

Crust:
1/4 cup butter
1-1/4 cups crushed vanilla wafers
1/4 cup ground walnuts

Filling:
1 lb. Neufchâtel cheese, softened
1-1/4 cups sour cream
1/3 cup packed light-brown sugar
2 eggs
1/2 cup coarsely chopped walnuts
2 tablespoons instant coffee granules
3 tablespoons boiling water

Garnish:
2/3 cup whipped cream
2/3 cup walnut halves
Chocolate candy coffee beans

Preheat oven to 350F (175C). Grease an 8-inch springform pan. To prepare crust, melt butter in a small saucepan over low heat. Stir in crushed vanilla wafers and walnuts. Press mixture in bottom of greased pan. Set aside. To prepare filling, beat Neufchâtel cheese, sour cream, brown sugar and eggs in a large bowl until smooth. Stir in walnuts. Dissolve coffee granules in boiling water; stir into cheese mixture. Spoon filling into prepared crust. Bake in preheated oven 45 minutes or until set. Cool before removing from pan. To garnish, whip cream until stiff. Pipe (with a pastry bag) a border of whipped cream rosettes around edge of cheesecake. Place walnut halves and candy coffee beans on alternate rosettes. Makes 8 to 10 servings.

—— GRANOLA CHEESECAKE ——

Crust:
1/4 cup butter
1 tablespoon light corn syrup
2 tablespoons brown sugar
2/3 cup regular rolled oats
3 tablespoons sunflower kernels
1 tablespoon slivered almonds
1 tablespoon All-Bran cereal

Filling:
8 oz. cream cheese, softened
1 cup cottage cheese, sieved
2 eggs
1/4 cup sugar
1/2 teaspoon vanilla extract
1 tablespoon all-purpose flour

Topping:
1/3 cup granola

Preheat oven to 375F (190C). Grease a 9-inch springform pan. To prepare crust, melt butter in a small saucepan over low heat. Stir in remaining crust ingredients. Press mixture in bottom of greased pan. Set aside. To prepare filling, beat cream cheese, cottage cheese, eggs, sugar, vanilla and flour in a large bowl until smooth. Spoon filling into prepared crust. Sprinkle with granola. Bake in preheated oven 40 minutes or until set. Cool before removing from pan. Makes 8 to 10 servings.

CHEESECAKE BARS

Crust:
1 recipe Special Cheesecake Pastry,
  page 12

Filling:
8 oz. cream cheese, softened
1 cup cottage cheese, sieved
2/3 cup sour cream
2 eggs
1/2 cup sugar
2 tablespoons semolina flour
2 tablespoons raisins
1/4 cup coarsely chopped glacé
  cherries
1/4 cup mixed candied citrus peel
1 tablespoon all-purpose flour
Finely grated peel and juice of 1
  orange

Glaze:
2 tablespoons apricot preserves
1 teaspoon water

Preheat oven to 325F (165C). Grease a 9-inch-square baking pan. To prepare crust, on a lightly floured surface, roll Special Cheesecake Pastry to 1/4-inch thickness. Using bottom of cake pan as a guide, cut dough to fit in bottom of pan. Line bottom of greased pan with dough. Set aside. To prepare filling, beat cream cheese, cottage cheese, sour cream, eggs, sugar and semolina flour in a large bowl until smooth. Combine fruits and toss with flour; stir into cheese mixture. Stir in orange peel and juice. Spoon filling onto prepared dough. Bake in preheated oven 1 hour or until set. To glaze, heat preserves and water in a small saucepan until liquified; brush over cheesecake. Cool completely before cutting. Makes 12 bars.

—— WINE & GRAPE CHEESECAKE ——

Crust:
1/3 cup butter
1-3/4 cups crushed vanilla wafers

Filling:
12 oz. cream cheese, softened
2 eggs
2 tablespoons sugar
2/3 cup sour cream
2 tablespoons all-purpose flour
2/3 cup dry white wine
1 lb. seedless green grapes

Preheat oven to 350F (175C). Grease a 9-inch springform pan. To prepare crust, melt butter in a small saucepan over low heat. Stir in crushed vanilla wafers. Press mixture in greased pan. Set aside. To prepare filling, beat cream cheese, eggs, sugar, sour cream and flour in a large bowl until smooth. Gradually beat in wine until smooth. Peel 1/3 of grapes, if desired. Stir the 1/3 of grapes into filling. Spoon filling into prepared crust. Bake in preheated oven 50 minutes or until set. Cool before removing from pan. To garnish, cut stem end off remaining grapes. Cover cheesecake with grapes. Makes 10 servings.

— GRAND MARNIER CHEESECAKE —

Crust:
1/3 cup butter
1-3/4 cups graham cracker crumbs

Filling:
1 lb. ricotta cheese
2/3 cup sour cream
3 eggs
1 tablespoon all-purpose flour
1/3 cup packed brown sugar
Finely grated peel and juice of 2
  oranges
1/3 cup Grand Marnier

Garnish:
2/3 cup whipping cream
1 orange
8 to 10 strawberries

Preheat oven to 350F (175C). Grease a 9-inch springform pan. To prepare crust, melt butter in a small saucepan over low heat. Stir in graham cracker crumbs. Press mixture in bottom of greased pan. Set aside. To prepare filling, beat ricotta cheese, sour cream, eggs, flour and brown sugar in a large bowl until smooth. Beat in orange juice and peel and Grand Marnier. Spoon filling into prepared crust. Bake in preheated oven 50 minutes or until set. Cool before removing from pan. To garnish, whip cream until stiff. Pipe (with a pastry bag) whipped cream rosettes around edge of cheesecake. Cut orange in 8 to 10 (1/4-inch-thick) slices. Cut each slice halfway through, twist and arrange around edge of cheesecake. Place a strawberry in each twist of orange. Makes 8 to 10 servings.

CAMPARI CHEESECAKE

Crust:
1/3 cup butter
1-3/4 cups graham cracker crumbs

Filling:
8 oz. Neufchâtel cheese, softened
2/3 cup plain yogurt
2/3 cup whipping cream
Finely grated peel and juice of 1 pink grapefruit
1/3 cup Campari
4 teaspoons unflavored gelatin
2 tablespoons water
2 eggs
1/4 cup sugar

Garnish:
2 pink grapefruit
2 kiwifruit
4 to 5 maraschino cherries, cut in half

Grease an 8-inch springform pan. To prepare crust, melt butter in a small saucepan over low heat. Stir in graham cracker crumbs. Press mixture in greased pan. Set aside. To prepare filling, beat Neufchâtel cheese, yogurt and whipping cream in a large bowl until smooth. Beat in grapefruit peel and juice and Campari. Combine gelatin and water in a small saucepan. Simmer until gelatin is completely dissolved; stir into cheese mixture. Beat eggs with sugar until they are thick and foamy and hold a ribbon when drawn across surface; fold into cheese mixture. Spoon filling into prepared crust. Refrigerate 2 to 3 hours or until set. Remove cheesecake from pan. To garnish, peel and cut grapefruit in segments. Peel and slice kiwifruit. Arrange grapefruit, kiwifruit and cherries around edge of cheesecake. Makes 8 to 10 servings.

———— PEAR & WINE CHEESECAKE ————

Topping:
2-1/2 cups red wine
3/4 cup sugar
1/2 teaspoon red food coloring
2-1/2 cups water
5 small pears, peeled

Crust:
1 recipe Special Cheesecake Pastry,
  page 12

Filling:
12 oz. cream cheese, softened
2 eggs
1/3 cup sugar
2/3 cup plain yogurt
2 tablespoons lemon juice
1/2 teaspoon ground cinnamon
Pinch of ground cloves
1 tablespoon all-purpose flour

To prepare topping, combine wine, sugar, food coloring and water in a large saucepan. Bring to a boil. Reduce heat, add pears and simmer 25 minutes or until pears are just tender. Cool pears in syrup while preparing cheesecake. Grease a 9-inch springform pan. To prepare crust, on a lightly floured surface, roll Special Cheesecake Pastry to a 1/4-inch thickness. Line greased pan with dough. Set aside. To prepare filling, beat cream cheese, eggs, sugar and yogurt in a large bowl until smooth. Beat in lemon juice, cinnamon, cloves and flour. Cut 2 pears in 1/2-inch pieces; stir into cheese mixture. Spoon filling into prepared crust. Bake in preheated oven 50 minutes or until set. Cool before removing from pan. Cut remaining pears in half, slice lengthwise and arrange in a fan shape on cheesecake. Makes 8 to 10 servings.

—— RUM & RAISIN CHEESECAKE ——

Filling:
1/2 cup raisins
1/3 cup dark rum
6 oz. cream cheese, softened
3/4 cup cottage cheese, sieved
2/3 cup whipping cream
2 eggs
1/4 cup packed brown sugar
1/2 teaspoon vanilla extract

Crust:
1/4 cup butter
1-1/4 cups graham cracker crumbs

To prepare filling, combine raisins and rum in a small bowl. Let stand at least 1 hour at room temperature. Preheat oven to 350F (175C). Grease an 8-inch springform pan. To prepare crust, melt butter in a small saucepan over low heat. Stir in graham cracker crumbs. Press mixture in greased pan. Set aside. Beat cream cheese, cottage cheese, whipping cream and eggs in a large bowl until smooth. Beat in brown sugar and vanilla. Stir in raisins and rum. Spoon filling into prepared crust. Bake in preheated oven 50 minutes or until set. Cool before removing from pan. This cheesecake is best eaten 2 days after baking. Makes 8 to 10 servings.

—— TUTTI FRUITI CHEESECAKE ——

12 oz. cream cheese, softened
1/4 cup sugar
2 eggs
1 tablespoon unflavored gelatin
2 tablespoons water
1/4 cup slivered almonds
2 tablespoons grated orange peel
2 tablespoons grated lemon peel
1/4 cup chopped raisins
3 tablespoons Grand Marnier or
    orange liqueur
1/4 cup chopped glacé cherries
28 to 30 ladyfinger cookies

Garnish:
5 glacé cherries, cut in half
Angelica pieces, cut in strips

Grease an 8" x 4" loaf pan. To pre-pare filling, beat cream cheese, sugar and eggs in a large bowl until smooth. Combine gelatin and water in a small saucepan. Simmer until gelatin is completely dissolved; stir into cheese mixture. Stir in almonds, orange and lemon peels, raisins, Grand Marnier or orange liqueur and cherries. Spoon filling into greased pan. Cut ladyfingers to fit into pan; arrange on filling. Refrigerate 2 to 3 hours or until set. Turn cheesecake out onto a serving dish. Garnish with cherry halves and angelica strips. Makes 10 servings.

TIPSY CHEESECAKE

Filling:
6 small macaroons, torn in pieces
1/3 cup dry sherry
6 oz. cream cheese, softened
3/4 cup cottage cheese, sieved
2/3 cup whipping cream
2 eggs
1/3 cup sugar
1 lb. raspberries

Crust:
1/3 cup butter
1-3/4 cup graham cracker crumbs

Garnish:
Powdered sugar

To prepare filling, combine macaroons and sherry in a small bowl. Soak 15 to 20 minutes or until sherry is absorbed. Preheat oven to 350F (175C). Grease an 8-inch springform pan. To prepare crust, melt butter in a small saucepan over low heat. Stir in graham cracker crumbs. Press mixture in bottom of greased pan. Set aside. Beat cream cheese, cottage cheese, whipping cream, eggs and sugar in a large bowl until smooth. Stir soaked macaroons into cheese mixture. Stir in 1/3 of raspberries. Spoon filling into prepared crust. Bake in preheated oven 50 minutes or until set. Cool before removing from pan. To garnish, dust with powdered sugar. Arrange remaining raspberries around edge of cheesecake. Makes 6 to 8 servings.

PERNOD CHEESECAKE

Crust:
1/4 cup butter
1-1/2 cups graham cracker crumbs

Filling:
7 oz. Neufchâtel cheese, softened
2/3 cup plain yogurt
2/3 cup whipping cream, whipped
2 tablespoons Pernod
4 teaspoons unflavored gelatin
3 tablespoons water
2 eggs
2 tablespoons honey
Finely grated peel of 1 orange

Garnish:
3 kiwifruit
2/3 cup whipping cream
1 small packet round plain chocolate
    wafers

Grease a 9-inch springform pan. To prepare crust, melt butter in a small saucepan over low heat. Stir in graham cracker crumbs. Press mixture in bottom of greased pan. Set aside. To prepare filling, beat Neufchâtel cheese and yogurt in a medium-size bowl until smooth. Fold in whipped cream and Pernod. Combine gelatin and water in a small saucepan. Simmer until gelatin is completely dissolved; stir into cheese mixture. Beat eggs, honey and orange peel until they are thick and foamy and hold a ribbon when drawn across surface; fold into cheese mixture. Spoon filling into prepared crust. Refrigerate 2 to 3 hours or until set. To garnish, peel and slice kiwifruit. Cut slices in half. Arrange around edge of cheesecake. Whip cream until stiff. Pipe (with a pastry bag) whipped cream between kiwifruit slices. Decorate with chocolate wafers. Makes 8 to 10 servings.

—— PIÑA COLADA CHEESECAKE ——

Crust:
1/3 cup butter
1-3/4 cups graham cracker crumbs

Filling:
12 oz. cream cheese, softened
2/3 cup sour cream
2/3 cup plain yogurt
2 eggs
1/3 cup sugar
1 tablespoon all-purpose flour
2 tablespoons creamed coconut
1/3 cup white rum
1 (20-oz.) can pineapple rings, drained
4 maraschino cherries, coarsely
  chopped

Topping:
2 egg whites
1/4 cup sugar
3 tablespoons shredded coconut
Maraschino cherries

Preheat oven to 350F (175C). Grease a 9-inch springform pan. To prepare crust, melt butter in a small saucepan over low heat. Stir in graham cracker crumbs. Press mixture in bottom of greased pan. Set aside. To prepare filling, beat cream cheese, sour cream, yogurt and eggs in a large bowl until smooth. Beat in sugar and flour. Stir coconut and rum into cheese mixture. Cut 3 pineapple rings in even-sized pieces; stir into cheese mixture with cherries. Spoon filling into prepared crust. Bake in preheated oven 45 minutes or until set. To prepare topping, beat egg whites with sugar until soft peaks form. Fold in coconut. Mound mixture on cheesecake. Cut remaining pineapple rings in wedges. Dot cheesecake with wedges. Decorate with cherries. Bake 7 to 12 minutes or until golden brown. Makes 8 to 10 servings.

– WHISKEY & GINGER CHEESECAKE –

Crust:
1/3 cup butter
1-3/4 cups crushed gingersnaps

Filling:
1 lb. cream cheese, softened
2/3 cup sour cream
2 eggs
1/3 cup packed brown sugar
1 tablespoon all-purpose flour
Finely grated peel and juice of 1
**   orange**
1 tablespoon chopped stem ginger
1/3 cup whiskey

Garnish:
2 tablespoons stem ginger
1 orange
4 cups water

Prepare oven to 350F (175C). Grease an 8-inch springform pan. To prepare crust, melt butter in a small saucepan over low heat. Stir in crushed gingersnaps. Press mixture in bottom of greased pan. Set aside. To prepare filling, beat cream cheese, sour cream and eggs in a large bowl until smooth. Beat in brown sugar, flour, orange peel and juice, ginger and whiskey. Spoon filling into prepared crust. Bake in preheated oven 50 minutes or until set. Cool before removing from pan. To garnish, slice ginger in thin rounds; arrange around edge of cheesecake. Peel orange (colored peel only) with a vegetable peeler. Combine peel and water in a medium-size saucepan. Simmer 3 to 4 minutes or until soft. Cut orange peel in thin strips. Wind each strip around a chop stick; remove chop stick. Arrange orange peel over ginger slices. Makes 8 to 10 servings.

CHOCOLATE MERINGUE CHEESECAKE

Chocolate Meringue Topping:
3 egg whites
2/3 cup sugar
2 tablespoons unsweetened cocoa
  powder

Crust:
1/3 cup melted butter
1-3/4 cups crushed gingersnaps

Filling:
1-1/2 lb. cream cheese, softened
1/4 cup packed brown sugar
3 eggs
Finely grated peel and juice of
  1 orange
1/2 teaspoon vanilla extract
2/3 cup whipping cream, whipped
7 oz. semisweet chocolate, broken in
  pieces

Garnish:
2/3 cup whipping cream
Powdered sugar

Preheat oven to 300F (150C). Line 2 baking sheets with parchment paper. To prepare meringue topping, beat egg whites with 2 tablespoons of sugar until stiff. Gradually add remaining sugar, beating until glossy. Sift cocoa over egg whites; fold in. Pipe (with a pastry bag fitted with a 1/2-inch nozzle) meringue in lengthwise strips on baking sheets. Bake with oven door slightly ajar 1-1/2 to 2 hours. Adjust oven to 375F (190C). To prepare crust, melt butter over low heat. Stir in gingersnaps. Press mixture in bottom of greased 9-inch springform pan. To prepare filling, beat cream cheese, brown sugar, eggs, orange peel and juice and vanilla until smooth. Bring cream to a boil; remove from heat. Stir in chocolate until melted; blend into cheese mixture. Spoon filling into crust. Bake 50 minutes or until set. Cool. To garnish, cover cheesecake with a thin layer of whipped cream. Break meringue in 1-1/2-inch pieces; place on cheesecake. Dust with powdered sugar. Makes 8 to 10 servings.

— WHITE CHOCOLATE & CHESTNUT — CHEESECAKE

Crust:
1/4 cup butter
1-3/4 cup crushed chocolate wafers

Filling:
12 oz. ricotta cheese
1 cup sweet chestnut puree
2/3 cup whipping cream
4 oz. white chocolate, broken in pieces
2 tablespoons cognac
3 eggs
1 tablespoon all-purpose flour

Garnish:
4 oz. white chocolate, grated
2/3 cup whipping cream
10 to 12 pieces candied chestnut
Sugar
Angelica pieces, cut in "leaves"

Preheat oven to 350F (175C). Grease an 8-inch springform pan. To prepare crust, melt butter in a small saucepan over low heat. Stir in crushed chocolate wafers. Press mixture in greased pan. Set aside. To prepare filling, beat ricotta cheese and chestnut puree in a medium-size bowl. Bring whipping cream to a boil in a small saucepan; remove from heat. Stir in chocolate until melted. Stir in cognac; blend into cheese mixture. Beat in eggs and flour until smooth. Spoon filling into prepared crust. Bake in preheated oven 1 hour or until set. Cool before removing from pan. To garnish, sprinkle white chocolate on cheesecake. Whip cream until stiff. Pipe (with a pastry bag) a border of 10 to 12 whipped cream rosettes around edge of cheesecake. Roll candied chestnuts in sugar; place in rosettes and decorate with angelica "leaves." Makes 10 to 12 servings.

—— CHOCOLATE & WHISKEY —— CHEESECAKE

Crust:
1/4 cup butter
1-3/4 cups crushed gingersnaps

Filling:
1-1/2 lb. cream cheese, softened
1/4 cup packed brown sugar
2 eggs
2 tablespoons unsweetened cocoa
powder
2 teaspoons ground ginger
2/3 cup whipping cream
8 oz. semisweet chocolate, broken in
pieces
1/3 cup whiskey

Garnish:
2 tablespoons unsweetened cocoa
powder
1 tablespoon plus 1 teaspoon
powdered sugar
1/2 teaspoon ground ginger

Preheat oven to 350F (175C). Grease an 8-inch springform pan. To prepare crust, melt butter in a small saucepan over low heat. Stir in crushed gingersnaps. Press mixture in bottom of greased pan. Set aside. To prepare filling, beat cream cheese, brown sugar, eggs, cocoa and ginger in a large bowl until smooth. Bring whipping cream to a boil in a small saucepan; remove from heat. Stir in chocolate until melted. Stir in whiskey; blend into cheese mixture. Spoon filling into prepared crust. Bake in preheated oven 45 minutes or until set. Cool before removing from pan. Cut 5 strips of waxed paper 3/4-inch wide. Lay strips 3/4 inch apart on cheesecake. To garnish, combine cocoa, powdered sugar and ginger in a small bowl; sift over cake. Carefully remove strips. Makes 8 to 10 servings.

—— KUMQUAT & CHOCOLATE ——
CHEESECAKE

Crust:
1/3 cup butter
2-1/2 cups crushed gingersnaps

Filling:
1-1/2 lb. ricotta cheese
1/4 cup packed dark-brown sugar
3 eggs
**Finely grated peel and juice of 1
   orange**
**1 teaspoon orange flower water, if
   desired**
2/3 cup whipping cream
**7 oz. semisweet chocolate, broken in
   pieces**

Garnish:
4 oz. kumquats
4 oz. semisweet chocolate shavings

Preheat oven to 350F (175C). Grease an 8-inch springform pan. To prepare crust, melt butter in a small saucepan over low heat. Stir in crushed gingersnaps. Press mixture in bottom of greased pan. Set aside. To prepare filling, beat ricotta cheese, brown sugar, eggs, orange peel and juice and orange flower water, if desired, in a large bowl until smooth. Bring whipping cream to a boil in a small saucepan; remove from heat. Stir in chocolate until melted; beat into cheese mixture until smooth. Spoon filling into prepared crust. Bake in preheated oven 45 minutes or until set. Cool before removing from pan. To garnish, slice kumquats thinly; arrange, with slices overlapping, around edge of cheesecake. Sprinkle cheesecake with chocolate shavings. Chill before serving. Makes 8 to 10 servings.

CHOCOLATE & PECAN CHEESECAKE

Crust:
1/4 cup butter
1-3/4 cups crushed vanilla wafers

Filling:
1-1/2 lb. ricotta cheese
2 tablespoons maple syrup
2 eggs
2/3 cup whipping cream
7 oz. semisweet chocolate, broken in pieces
3/4 cup coarsely chopped pecans

Garnish:
3/4 cup pecan halves
3 oz. semisweet chocolate, grated
Powdered sugar

Preheat oven to 350F (175C). Grease an 8-inch springform pan. To prepare crust, melt butter in a small saucepan over low heat. Stir in crushed vanilla wafers. Press mixture in bottom of greased pan. Set aside. To prepare filling, beat ricotta cheese, maple syrup and eggs in a large bowl until smooth. Bring whipping cream to a boil in a small saucepan; remove from heat. Stir in chocolate until melted; blend into cheese mixture. Stir in pecans. Spoon filling into prepared crust. Bake in preheated oven 45 minutes or until set. Cool before removing from pan. To garnish, arrange pecans around edge of cheesecake. Sprinkle with grated chocolate. Dust grated chocolate with powdered sugar. Makes 8 to 10 servings.

─RICH CHOCOLATE CHEESECAKE─

Crust:
1/3 cup butter
1-3/4 cups crushed chocolate wafers

Filling:
1-1/2 lb. cream cheese, softened
3 eggs
1/4 cup packed dark-brown sugar
3 tablespoons molasses
2 tablespoons unsweetened cocoa
   powder
1 teaspoon ground allspice
Finely grated peel and juice of 1
   orange
2/3 cup whipping cream
8 oz. semisweet chocolate, broken in
   pieces
1/4 cup unsalted butter

Garnish:
8 oz. semisweet chocolate shavings
4 oz. white chocolate shavings

Preheat oven to 350F (175C). Grease a 9-inch springform pan. To prepare crust, melt butter in a small saucepan over low heat. Stir in crushed chocolate wafers. Press mixture in bottom of greased pan. Set aside. To prepare filling, beat cream cheese, eggs, brown sugar, molasses, cocoa, allspice and orange peel and juice in a large bowl until smooth. Bring whipping cream to a boil in a small saucepan; remove from heat. Stir in chocolate and butter until melted; beat into cheese mixture until smooth. Spoon filling into prepared crust. Bake in preheated oven 50 minutes or until set. Cool completely before removing from pan. Garnish with chocolate shavings, alternating dark and white chocolate. Makes 10 to 12 servings.

FUDGENUT & RAISIN CHEESECAKE

Crust:
1/4 cup butter
1-3/4 cups crushed gingersnaps

Filling:
1-1/2 lb. cream cheese, softened
1/4 cup packed dark-brown sugar
3 eggs
2/3 cup whipping cream
7 oz. semisweet chocolate, broken in
   pieces
1/2 cup chopped mixed nuts
1/3 cup chopped raisins

Garnish:
Powdered sugar

Preheat oven to 350F (175C). Grease a 9-inch springform pan. To prepare crust, melt butter in a small saucepan over low heat. Stir in crushed gingersnaps. Press mixture in bottom of greased pan. Set aside. To prepare filling, beat cream cheese, brown sugar and eggs in a large bowl until smooth. Bring whipping cream to a boil in a small saucepan; remove from heat. Stir in chocolate until melted; blend into cheese mixture. Stir in nuts and raisins. Spoon filling into prepared crust. Bake in preheated oven 50 minutes or until set. Cool before removing from pan. To garnish, dust with powdered sugar. Makes 10 to 12 servings.

— CHOCOLATE & ORANGE TERRINE —

Filling:
12 oz. ricotta cheese
2 tablespoons dark-brown sugar
1 egg
Finely grated peel and juice of 1 orange
2/3 cup whipping cream
6 oz. semisweet chocolate, broken in pieces

Crust:
1/2 recipe Special Cheesecake Pastry, page 12

Garnish:
3 to 4 drops orange food coloring
2 oz. marzipan
6 to 8 cloves
2/3 cup whipping cream

Preheat oven to 350F (175C). Grease an 8" x 4" loaf pan and line with waxed paper. To prepare filling, beat ricotta cheese, brown sugar, egg and orange peel and juice in a large bowl until smooth. Bring whipping cream to a boil in a small saucepan; remove from heat. Stir in chocolate until melted; blend into cheese mixture. Spoon filling into prepared pan. Bake in preheated oven 20 minutes. Meanwhile, to prepare crust, on a lightly floured surface, roll Special Cheesecake Pastry to a 1/4-inch-thick rectangle same size as top of pan. Lay dough over partially-baked cheese-cake and crimp edges. Bake 20 minutes more. Cool before removing from pan. To garnish, knead food coloring into marzipan. Shape in 6 to 8 small balls. Roll on a fine cheese grater to simulate orange skin. Push a clove into top of each "orange." Whip cream until stiff. Pipe (with a pastry bag) a whipped cream rosette on each serving. Place an "orange" in each rosette. Makes 6 to 8 servings.

CHOCOLATE & HONEY CHEESECAKE

Crust:
1/3 cup butter
1-3/4 cups crushed vanilla wafers

Filling:
1-1/2 lb. ricotta cheese
2 tablespoons honey
2 eggs
2/3 cup whipping cream
**1 (7-oz.) Toblerone Almond &
Chocolate candy bar, broken in
pieces**

Topping:
2 tablespoons honey
1 cup granola
Powdered sugar

Preheat oven to 350F (175C). Grease a 9-inch springform pan. To prepare crust, melt butter in a small saucepan over low heat. Stir in crushed vanilla wafers. Press mixture in bottom of greased pan. Set aside. To prepare filling, beat ricotta cheese, honey and eggs in a medium-size bowl until smooth. Bring whipping cream to a boil in a small saucepan. Remove from heat. Stir in chocolate until melted; blend into cheese mixture. Bake in preheated oven 30 minutes. To make topping, melt honey in a small saucepan over low heat. Stir in granola. Spread on partially-baked cheesecake. Bake 15 minutes more. Cool before removing from pan. Dust with powdered sugar. Makes 10 to 12 servings.

CARDAMOM & LIME CHEESECAKE

Crust:
1 recipe Chocolate Stripe Spongecake
  Border, page 11
1/3 cup butter
1-3/4 cups crushed vanilla wafers

Filling:
1 lb. Neufchâtel cheese, softened
1-1/4 cups plain yogurt
3 eggs, separated
1/3 cup sugar
3/4 teaspoon ground cardamon
Finely grated peel and juice of 3 limes
1 tablespoon plus 1 teaspoon
  unflavored gelatin
3 tablespoons water

Garnish:
3 limes
2/3 cup whipping cream

Grease bottom of a 9-inch spring-form pan. To prepare crust, cut Chocolate Stripe Spongecake Border to same height of greased pan; wrap strips around sides of pan. Melt butter in a small saucepan over low heat. Stir in crushed vanilla wafers. Press mixture in bottom of greased pan. Set aside. To prepare filling, beat Neufchâtel cheese, yogurt, egg yolks and 1 tablespoon of sugar until smooth. Beat in cardamom and lime peel and juice. Combine gelatin and water in a small saucepan. Simmer until gelatin is completely dissolved; beat into cheese mixture. Beat egg whites with remaining sugar until soft peaks form; fold into cheese mixture. Spoon filling into prepared crust. Refrigerate 2 to 3 hours or until set. Trim spongecake border level with cheesecake. To garnish, slice limes in 1/4-inch-thick slices. Cut each lime slice halfway through, twist and arrange around edge of cheesecake. Whip cream until stiff. Pipe (with pastry bag) whipped cream rosettes between twists of lime. Makes 8 to 10 servings.

GEORGE HANDLEY CHEESECAKE

Topping:
1-3/4 cups boiling water
3 small oranges, cut in 1/8-inch slices
1/4 cup packed light-brown sugar
5 tablespoons honey
2 whole cloves
1 (3-inch) cinnamon stick
1/2 bay leaf
5 allspice berries

Crust:
1/3 cup butter
1-3/4 cup crushed gingersnaps

Filling:
1 lb. cream cheese, softened
3 eggs
1/3 cup sugar
1 tablespoon all-purpose flour
1/3 cup golden raisins

To prepare topping, combine boiling water and oranges in a large saucepan. Add brown sugar, 2 tablespoons of honey and spices. Cover and simmer 20 to 25 minutes or until orange slices are tender; drain on a wire rack. Meanwhile, preheat oven to 350F (175C). Grease an 8-inch springform pan. To prepare crust, melt butter in a small saucepan over low heat. Stir in crushed gingersnaps. Press mixture in greased pan. Set aside. To prepare filling, beat ricotta cheese, eggs, sugar and flour in a large bowl until smooth. Stir in raisins. Spoon filling into prepared crust. Bake in preheated oven 45 minutes or until set. To garnish, arrange orange slices on cheesecake. Cool before removing from pan. Heat remaining honey in small saucepan until liquified. Brush honey over orange slices. Makes 8 to 10 servings.

—— SPICED HONEY CHEESECAKE ——

Crust:
1 recipe Sweet Shortcrust Pastry,
  page 13

Filling:
1 lb. Neufchâtel cheese, softened
1-1/4 cups plain yogurt
1/4 cup honey
3 eggs
1 teaspoon ground cinnamon
1/4 teaspoon ground allspice
Pinch of ground cloves

Glaze:
1 cup orange juice
1 tablespoon honey
2 tablespoons cornstarch
3 tablespoons water

Garnish:
Orange peel strips

Preheat oven to 350F (175C). Grease an 8-inch springform pan. To prepare crust, on a lightly floured surface, roll Sweet Shortcrust Pastry to a 1/4-inch thickness. Line bottom and 2 inches up sides of greased pan with dough. Refrigerate while preparing filling. To prepare filling, beat Neufchâtel cheese, yogurt, honey and eggs in a large bowl until smooth. Beat in spices. Spoon filling into prepared dough. Bake in preheated oven 45 minutes or until set. To glaze, combine orange juice and honey in a small saucepan. Bring to a boil. Combine cornstarch and water; stir into orange-juice mixture. Simmer until thickened. Pour over cheesecake. Garnish with strips of orange peel. Cool and refrigerate 2 to 3 hours or until topping is set. Makes 6 to 8 servings.

— BANANA & LIME CHEESECAKE —

Crust:
1/3 cup butter
1-3/4 cups crushed gingersnaps
1/2 teaspoon ground allspice

Filling:
1 lb. cream cheese, softened
1/3 cup plus 2 tablespoons packed
   light-brown sugar
Finely grated peel and juice of 2 limes
2 ripe bananas, mashed
2 eggs, separated

Garnish:
3 bananas
2 tablespoons lemon juice
Lime peel strips

Preheat oven to 350F (175C). Grease a 9-inch springform pan. To prepare crust, melt butter in a small saucepan over low heat. Stir in crushed gingersnaps and allspice. Press mixture in bottom of greased pan. Set aside. To prepare filling, beat cream cheese, 1/3 cup of brown sugar, lime peel and juice, bananas and egg yolks in a large bowl until smooth. Beat egg whites and remaining brown sugar until soft peaks form; fold into cheese mixture. Spoon filling into prepared crust. Bake in preheated oven 1 hour. Cool completely. To garnish, slice bananas diagonally in ovals and toss gently with lemon juice. Overlap banana slices around edge of cheesecake. Decorate with strips of lime peel. Makes 8 to 10 servings.

—— CHEESE & CELERY CAKE ——

Crust:
1/3 cup butter
2-1/2 cups graham cracker crumbs
1/2 cup ground walnuts

Filling:
1 lb. ricotta cheese
1/2 cup sour cream
2 eggs
1 tablespoon all-purpose flour
Salt and pepper to taste
1/2 cup chopped celery
3/4 cup coarsely chopped walnuts

Garnish:
6 to 8 celery stalks, cut in 2-1/2-inch
  strips
1/3 cup walnut halves

Preheat oven to 350F (175C). Grease a 7-inch springform pan. To prepare crust, melt butter in a small saucepan over low heat. Stir in graham cracker crumbs and walnuts. Press mixture in greased pan. Set aside. To prepare filling, process ricotta cheese, sour cream, eggs, flour and salt and pepper in a blender or food processor until smooth. Stir in celery and walnuts. Spoon filling into prepared crust. Bake in preheated oven 50 minutes or until set. Cool before removing from pan. To garnish, arrange celery strips in a fan shape around edge of cheesecake. Decorate with walnut halves. Makes 6 to 8 servings.

—————— HERB & GARLIC MOLD ——————

1 lb. cottage cheese, sieved
3 oz. cream cheese, softened
1/2 cup sour cream
3 garlic cloves, crushed
2 tablespoons chopped fresh parsley
2 tablespoons chopped fresh thyme
Freshly ground pepper to taste

Garnish:
3 tablespoons chopped fresh parsley
1 tomato rose

Line a large wire strainer with a double layer of cheesecloth or muslin. Beat cottage cheese, cream cheese and sour cream in a large bowl until smooth. Stir in garlic, parsley, thyme and pepper. Spoon mixture into prepared wire strainer and place over a bowl. Refrigerate overnight while mixture drains. Turn mold out on a flat surface. To garnish, roll mold in parsley. Decorate with tomato rose. Makes 6 to 8 servings.

—— HAM & MUSHROOM TERRINE ——

1 oz. Westphalian or Black Forest
   ham, thinly sliced
3 tablespoons butter
1 small onion, chopped
1 tablespoon all-purpose flour
1/2 cup milk
2 egg yolks
Freshly ground pepper to taste
8 oz. ricotta cheese
2 oz. Westphalian or Black Forest
   ham, chopped
1 cup button mushrooms

Garnish:
Fresh mushrooms
Sprigs fresh parsley

Grease a 9-inch terrine or loaf pan
with a 3-cup capacity. Line bottom
and 2 long sides with waxed paper.
Line prepared pan with ham slices.
Set aside. Melt butter in a small skillet
over medium heat. Add onion and
cook until onion begins to soften. Stir
in flour; cook 1 to 2 minutes. Gradually add milk, stirring until thickened. Whisk in egg yolks and pepper.
Remove from heat and cool. In a
blender or food processor, process
sauce and ricotta cheese until
smooth. Stir in chopped ham. Cover
mushrooms with boiling water in a
small bowl. Let stand 2 to 3 minutes.
Drain and stir into cheese mixture.
Spoon filling into greased pan. Refrigerate 2 hours. To garnish, cut
mushrooms in half. Decorate with
mushroom halves and sprigs of parsley. Makes 6 to 8 servings.

—— CRANBERRY-TURKEY BAKE ——

Crust:
1 (3-oz.) pkg. stuffing mix

Filling:
2 tablespoons butter
1 medium-size onion, chopped
1 lb. ricotta cheese
3 eggs
1 tablespoon all-purpose flour
Salt and pepper to taste
2 tablespoons chopped fresh chives
1 cup coarsely chopped cooked turkey

Topping:
1 cup cranberries
1/2 cup orange juice
1 tablespoons sugar
2 tablespoons cornstarch
1 tablespoon water

Garnish:
Fresh holly leaves

Preheat oven to 350F (175C). To prepare crust, prepare stuffing mix according to package directions. Press stuffing in bottom and 1-1/2 inches up sides of an 8-inch springform pan. Set aside. To prepare filling, melt butter in a medium-size skillet. Add onion and cook until onion is soft; cool. Beat ricotta cheese, eggs, flour, salt and pepper in a blender or food processor until smooth. Stir onion, chives and turkey into cheese mixture. Spoon filling into prepared crust. Bake in preheated oven 50 minutes or until set. Cool before removing from pan. To prepare topping, combine cranberries, orange juice and sugar in a small saucepan. Bring to a boil and simmer about 5 minutes or until berries pop. Combine cornstarch and water. Stir into cranberries and simmer until thick; spread on cheesecake. Cool completely. Garnish with holly leaves. Makes 6 to 8 servings.

— CHEESE STUFFED POTATOES —

24 new potatoes
4 oz. cream cheese
1/2 cup sour cream
2 tablespoons chopped fresh chives
Juice of 1/2 lemon
Pinch of cayenne pepper

Garnish:
1/3 cup lumpfish caviar
1 bunch fresh chervil
1 lemon, cut in 24 wedges

Boil potatoes in a large saucepan of salted water 20 minutes or until tender. Drain and cool under cold running water. Set aside. Beat cream cheese and sour cream in a small bowl until smooth. Stir in chives, lemon juice and cayenne pepper. Cut tops from potatoes. Scoop out pulp; reserve for another use. Fill potato cavity with cheese mixture. To garnish, top each potato with a dollop of lumpfish caviar. Garnish each with a sprig of chervil and a lemon wedge. Makes 24 stuffed pototes.

—— SMOKED TROUT TERRINE ——

Aspic:
1 tablespoon unflavored gelatin
2 cups fish, veal or chicken stock
1 tablespoon plus 1-1/2 teaspoons
  lemon juice
1 lemon, thinly sliced
2 tomatoes, sliced
Fresh dill sprigs

Filling:
12 oz. smoked trout, boned
2 oz. cream cheese, softened
2 oz. cottage cheese, sieved
1/4 cup butter, softened
Juice of 1 lemon
Pinch of cayenne pepper
Pinch of ground mace
1 tablespoon chopped fresh parsley

Place an 8-inch rectangular terrine or gelatin mold in freezer 10 minutes. To prepare aspic, combine gelatin and 1/2 cup of stock in a small saucepan. Simmer until gelatin is completely dissolved. Stir in remaining stock and lemon juice. Pour into a medium-size bowl and refrigerate until slightly thickened. Coat inside of terrine with a small amount of aspic. Place 6 lemon slices in bottom of terrine. Arrange tomato slices between lemon slices. Place sprigs of dill along sides of terrine. Reserve remaining lemon and tomato slices and sprigs of dill to garnish finished terrine. If bowl of aspic has set, place over a saucepan of boiling water a few seconds; stir until melted. Coat bottom and sides of terrine with a second layer of aspic. Refrigerate while preparing filling. To prepare filling, process trout, cream cheese, cottage cheese, butter, lemon juice, cayenne pepper and mace in a blender or food processor until smooth. Stir in parsley. Spoon filling over aspic. Refrigerate 1 hour or until firm. To remove terrine from mold, place mold in a bowl of hot water 15 seconds. Place serving dish over mold and invert; remove mold. Garnish with reserved lemon and tomato slices and sprigs of dill. Makes 6 to 8 servings.

———— SWISS CHEESE TARTS ————

Crust:
**1 recipe Sweet Shortcrust Pastry,
    page 13**

Filling:
1/3 cup milk
1/3 cup whipping cream
2 teaspoons all-purpose flour
1 egg
1/2 cup shredded Gruyère cheese
1/4 cup grated Parmesan cheese
1 tablespoon kirsch
Freshly ground pepper to taste
Pinch of grated nutmeg

Garnish:
Sprigs fresh parsley

Preheat oven to 425F (220C). Grease 12 tartlet pans. To prepare crust, on a lightly floured surface, roll Sweet Shortcrust Pastry as thinly as possible. Cut out 12 circles with a fluted cutter 1-inch larger than pans. Line greased pans with dough. Refrigerate while preparing filling. To prepare filling, combine milk and whipping cream in a medium-size bowl. Sprinkle with flour and stir well. Beat in egg, cheeses, kirsch, pepper and nutmeg. Spoon filling into prepared shells. Bake in preheated oven on top rack 12 to 15 minutes or until risen. Garnish with sprigs of parsley and serve at once. Makes 12 servings.

—— TARAMASALATA ROULADE ——

2 tablespoons butter
8 oz. fresh spinach, washed, drained, chopped
Pinch of grated nutmeg
Salt and pepper to taste
3 eggs, separated
1 tablespoon all-purpose flour
2 tablespoons grated Parmesan cheese

Filling:
8 oz. ricotta cheese
4 oz. taramasalata

Garnish:
Tomato slices
Hard-boiled egg slices
Fresh parsley sprigs

Preheat oven to 400F (205C). Grease a baking sheet and line with parchment paper. Melt butter in a medium-size saucepan over medium heat. Stir in spinach and cook 3 to 4 minutes or until spinach wilts. Stir in nutmeg, salt and pepper. Combine egg yolks, flour and Parmesan cheese in a small bowl; stir into spinach mixture. Beat egg whites until soft peaks form; fold into spinach mixture. Spread mixture on prepared baking sheet. Bake in preheated oven on top rack 12 minutes or until springy to touch. Remove from oven, cover with a tea towel and cool. To prepare filling, beat ricotta cheese and taramasalata in a medium-size bowl until smooth. Spread filling over spinach roulade and roll up, jelly-roll fashion; cut in 1-inch slices. Garnish with tomato and egg slices and sprigs of parsley. Makes 6 servings.

— TORTE DE FROMAGE AU CHEVRE —

Crust:
1/4 cup butter
3/4 cup bulgur wheat
3 tablespoons sunflower kernels

Filling:
1/2 cup golden raisins
3 tablespoons sweet white wine
3 oz. goat cheese
6 oz. cottage cheese, sieved
2 eggs
Pinch of cayenne pepper
1 tablespoon unflavored gelatin
2 tablespoons water
2/3 cup whipping cream, whipped

Garnish:
1-1/4 cups seedless green grapes

Grease an 8-inch springform pan and line with waxed paper. To prepare crust, melt butter in a small saucepan over low heat. Stir in bulgur wheat and sunflower kernels. Press mixture in bottom of prepared pan. Set aside. To prepare filling, combine raisins and wine in a small saucepan. Simmer until wine is absorbed. Beat goat cheese, cottage cheese, eggs and cayenne pepper in a medium-size bowl until light. Combine gelatin and water in a small saucepan. Simmer until gelatin is completely dissolved; stir into cheese mixture. Stir in raisins and wine. Fold whipped cream into cheese mixture. Spoon filling over prepared crust. Refrigerate 2 to 3 hours or until set. Remove from pan. To garnish, cut stem ends from grapes. Cover cheesecake with grapes. Makes 6 servings.

———— TURKISH BOUREKAS ————

12 oz. feta cheese
2 eggs
1/4 cup fresh bread crumbs
3 tablespoons chopped fresh parsley
Freshly ground pepper to taste
6 sheets filo pastry
3/4 cup butter, melted
4 small tomatoes, sliced
3 tablespoons sesame seeds
3 tablespoons poppy seeds

Garnish:
Tomato slices
Fresh parsley sprigs

Preheat oven to 400F (205F). Lightly grease a baking sheet. To prepare filling, crumble feta cheese into a large bowl. Stir in 1 egg, bread crumbs, parsley and pepper. Set aside. Lay 1 sheet of filo pastry on a flat surface. Keep remainder covered with a damp cloth. Cut in 24 (3-inch-wide) strips. Cover strips with another damp towel to prevent drying. Brush 1 strip of pastry with melted butter. Place 1 tomato slice at end of strip, followed by 1 spoonful of filling. Fold strip end over end, as if folding a flag, to form a triangle. Continue folding until complete length of pastry has been folded. Repeat using remaining pastry strips and filling. Place bourekas on greased baking sheet. Beat remaining egg; brush bourekas with beaten egg. Sprinkle 1/2 of bourekas with sesame seeds and remainder with poppy seeds. Bake in preheated oven 25 minutes or until golden brown. Garnish with tomato slices and sprigs of parsley. Makes 24 bourekas.

Variation
Prepare cocktail bourekas by reducing width of pastry strips to 2 inches.

Strawberry Smooth Cake, page 48

Raspberry Cheesecake, page 68

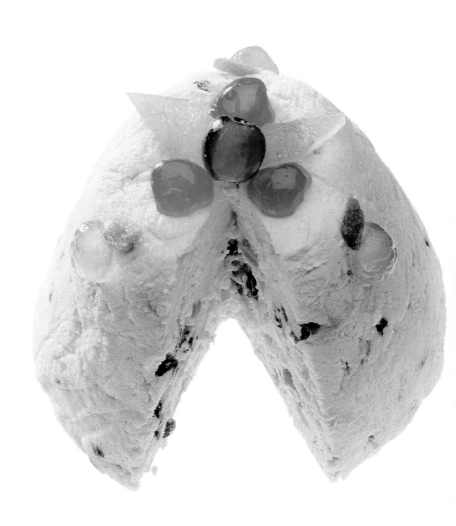

Paskha, page 20

Chocolate & Orange Terrine, page 98

Smoked Trout Terrine, 109

Taramasalata Roulade, page 111

INDEX